THE UNIVE           ARY

# COLOURS OF WAR
## War Art 1939-45

# ALAN ROSS

# COLOURS OF WAR
## *War Art 1939–45*

With a Foreword by Kenneth Clark

JONATHAN CAPE
THIRTY BEDFORD SQUARE LONDON

For Leonard Rosoman

This book has been
published with financial
assistance from the
Arts Council of Great Britain.

First published 1983
Copyright © 1983 by Alan Ross
Foreword © 1983 by Kenneth Clark
Jonathan Cape Ltd, 30 Bedford Square, London WC1

British Library Cataloguing in Publication Data
Ross, Alan
    Colours of war.
    1. World War, 1939 — 1945 — Art and the War —
    History and criticism
    I. Title
    940.54'8      D811.5

ISBN 0-224-02038-2

Printed in Great Britain by Jolly & Barber Ltd, Rugby

# Contents

Ravenous Time has flowers for his food
in Autumn, yet can cleverly make good
each petal; devours animals and men,
but for the dead he can create ten.
    Keith Douglas, from *Time Eating*


Art is an instrument of war; for use
as a weapon of defence and attack against
the enemy.
                    Pablo Picasso

# Foreword

*by Kenneth Clark*

My very earliest experience of what could be called modern art took place, paradoxically enough, in the Royal Academy, when in 1916 was held an exhibition of pictures commissioned for Canada under the aegis of Lord Beaverbrook. Beaverbrook himself had no interest in modern art, but he had taken on as an adviser a critic called P. G. Konody, who had a considerable reputation at the time, and Konody had had the good idea of using a grant from the Beaverbrook Foundation to form a collection of modern English artists for the National Gallery of Canada. The collection still exists, and can be seen in a cellar in Ottawa by anyone who has the influence and tenacity to get the cellar opened. The selection of artists showed excellent judgment, and it contains one masterpiece, Augustus John's huge cartoon *The Kensingtons at La Bassae*, which may eventually prove to be the finest thing he ever did.

I mention all this because it was with this exhibition still in my mind that, on the first day of the war, in 1939, I went round to the Treasury to ask if I might be allowed to submit plans for a similar scheme. In those early days the answer was usually *yes* (later on in the war it would almost certainly have been *no*), and I set about the plans which are described in this book. I had two pieces of good fortune. First of all I was able to operate through the Ministry of Information, of which I was a senior member; and secondly I discovered the ideal secretary to a War Artists' Advisory Committee, named E. M. O'R. Dickey, who was himself a member of the Treasury, but in his youth had been an able painter. It is through Dickey's understanding of artists and tireless attention to detail that the collection achieved its quality.

An obvious problem was how the artists should be chosen; and here I had a good idea. It could be argued that there were four participants in the scheme — Air Ministry, Admiralty, War Office and Home Office. Why not allow each of these government departments to send a representative to a central committee, who could tell this body what it required, and arrange for the artists in question to secure the necessary permits? This had the immediate advantage of keeping out some official bodies who might feel that they ought really to be running the whole scheme themselves. The choice of representatives was not as difficult as it might seem, since each of the government departments had one or two members with artistic leanings whose talents they were glad to have usefully employed. I must confess that I visited the heads of these departments with some knowledge of their staff, and my suggestions of names were gratefully accepted. In this way we formed a core for our committee, which met for over a hundred meetings without an angry word. We had representatives of the Royal College of Art and the Slade (both of them humane and co-operative people). And we had Muirhead Bone as a link with the artists' committee of the First World War, and no one ever had a more loyal supporter.

In one important respect the artists of the Second World War differed basically from those of the First. In the first war our imagination was dominated by our awareness of the terrible sufferings of life in the trenches in France. The occasional air raid in London, although frightening and inconvenient, was obviously no more than a sideshow and was dismissed as such. In the Second World War hostilities had spread everywhere, and there was no such thing as 'a front', or rather there were half-a-dozen fronts of more or less equal importance. From the artists' point of view this had a certain advantage, as they could be asked to go to places that had a special interest to them. Moreover, the most important 'front' was at home, particularly in London, which offered two contrasting subjects to the artist: first the scenes of destruction varying from grandiose deserts, like the surroundings of St Paul's Cathedral, to the poor streets in Whitechapel or Battersea, which placed on record a degree of squalor and misery which is usually overlooked except by social reformers.

With this wide range of subject matter there were themes for artists of all kinds, ranging from Graham Sutherland and John Piper, who looked for the squalor of the slums and their pitiful associations, to Schwabe and Muirhead Bone himself, who depicted the contrast between famous buildings half destroyed by bombing and fire and the wretched hovels lying behind them which war damage had revealed. This was an English, more particularly a London scene. The London air raids of the First World War had been regarded as a sort of joke (although I found them alarming enough), and my parents did not bother to move me down to the country. In the Second World War London was for almost a year the chief focus of attack. Goering had boasted that six months' bombing would bring London to her knees, and he was not so far wrong. Only those who saw the weekly reports of the Ministry of Information knew how strong a peace party existed behind closed doors.

All those interested in keeping a fair record of the artistic climate of the present half century must be grateful to Mr Alan Ross for having set down this account of the war artists of the Second World War. Such events are soon forgotten when those who have taken part in them have vanished from the scene, but the historians of that period will turn indignantly to those who witnessed such happenings and failed to make a record of them. Mr Ross's diligence and thoroughness will then seem more valuable than a quantity of speculation.

# *Preface*

I have chosen, out of the various alternatives, the biographical approach to a study of British war art between 1939 and 1945 – dividing the war into various zones and describing the art relating to them through the artist's attitude to his experience and as much as possible by reference to his own statements and circumstances. There were over 5,500 paintings produced as a result of the War Artists' scheme and I have tried as far as circumstances allow to reproduce what seems to me the best of them. There are also some which were painted independently of the scheme. There is no attempt to represent all aspects of the war equally. The pictures in a sense chose themselves: they were those that, after repeated siftings, most held the attention by reason of qualities, formal and visionary, beyond the merely literal. Artistic merit was the criterion by which the War Artists' Advisory Committee accepted or rejected work, not illustrative accuracy. What follows is the war of 1939–45 as experienced by a number of painters working on different tasks and in different places. The images are what count, the text essentially the attempt to situate them and describe how they came into being. Inevitably, the war was more important for some painters than for others, but in the most successful works the painter has absorbed the subject to an extent that it ceases to seem like a commission.

The news of Eric Ravilious's disappearance off the coast of Iceland reached me shortly before I myself sailed from Seydisfiord on a Murmansk-bound convoy. His work was already familiar to me and his death was shattering. For someone like myself, involved in trying to write poetry during five years of war, it has been an educative and fascinating exercise learning how painters set about their task in similar conditions. Many of the paintings in this book have been part of my experience since they were first shown at the National Gallery and elsewhere during the war. Others have been a delight and a surprise to come upon all these years later.

My thanks must go to Joseph Darracott and Angela Weight, successively Keepers, Department of Art, Imperial War Museum, for their help and encouragement. Also to their staff, in particular Vivienne Crawford, Jennifer Wood and Michael Moody, for their courteous assistance.

October 1982                                                                                      A.R.

# Introduction

Not only how far away, but the way that you say it
Is very important. Perhaps you may never get
The knack of judging a distance, but at least you know
How to report on a landscape: the central sector,
The right of arc and that, which we had last Tuesday,
     And at least you know

That maps are of time, not place, so far as the army
Happens to be concerned—the reason being,
Is one which need not delay us. Again, you know
There are three kinds of tree, three only, the fir and the poplar
And those which have bushy tops to; and lastly
     That things only seem to be things

Henry Reed, *Judging Distances*

Artists have always accompanied armies and recorded their doings. Sometimes they have been in the front line, sometimes at a safe distance. Their purpose and their motives have been varied, as have been their styles: allegorical, symbolical, illustrative, documentary. They have painted to celebrate, to honour, to mourn, to protest, to warn, to record. However, the way in which artists have gone about their business in relation to war—from Paolo Uccello in the mid-fifteenth century, through Leonardo da Vinci, Altdorfer, the brothers Pollaiuolo, Michelangelo, Dürer and Bruegel to Rubens a century later; from Velazquez and Tintoretto to David and Goya in the eighteenth century; from Delacroix and Géricault at the beginning of the nineteenth century to Manet and Rousseau at the end of it; from, in our own century, Marc, Macke, Dix and Grosz to Nevinson, Wyndham Lewis and Picasso—this is outside the scope of this book. The celebrated painters I have mentioned are only a few who have recorded aspects of war: there were those who painted battles in India and the Far East, the feats of Moghul emperors, Japanese warlords, Napoleon's triumphs, British colonisers, American civil war engagements, the deeds of Nelson and Wellington.

*opposite: above,*
NEVINSON, C.R.W.,
*Marching Men,* 1916,
Gouache, $5\frac{1}{2} \times 8$ ins;

*below,* LEWIS, Wyndham,
*A Battery Shelled,* 1918,
Oil, $72 \times 125$ ins

In relation to these the Second World War, as it appears in the art of the period, is inevitably circumscribed; not only by the nature of contemporary warfare but by the situation in art. The powerful, mannered paintings of the First World War by Gertler, Nevinson, Wyndham Lewis and Bomberg—works such as Gertler's *The Merry Go Round*, Nevinson's *La Mitrailleuse* and *Returning to the Trenches*, Lewis's *A Battery Shelled* and Bomberg's *Sappers at Work*—were all done under the influence of Cubism, when the principles and definitions of Futurism and Vorticism were being violently debated by their protagonists. Similarly, the best work of Paul Nash—*The Menin Road*, *Vimy Ridge*, *Void* and *We are Making a New World*—of John Nash, *Over the Top*, and Stanley Spencer, *Travoys Arriving with Wounded*, conveying the same sensations of devastation, loss and waste as those expressed in the poems of Sassoon, Owen and Blunden, were more essentially modern in feeling and technique than most war pictures done twenty-five years later.

The later work of Nevinson was altogether milder and more conventional, and Bomberg painted between the wars in essentially naturalistic terms. Edward Wadsworth, another leading Vorticist, responsible for some elegant woodcuts done in the Aegean, where he was serving as an R.N.V.R. officer in Naval Intelligence, as well as the monumental painting *Dazzle—Ships in Dry Dock at Liverpool*, never reappeared as a war artist, though in 1939 he was still only 50. Wadsworth had been closely involved, after he had been invalided home from the Eastern Mediterranean in 1917, in supervising the camouflage of warships, mainly at Bristol and Liverpool, where he was responsible for over 2,000 ships. Wadsworth's Greek experience and his work in camouflage were seen to be more or less of a piece in the superb series of prints he showed in 1919, some of them Vorticist renderings of machinery and walled Mediterranean towns, some camouflaged warships in dry dock. After the war he, too, retreated from Vorticism into a more naturalistic style, a style in which still-lifes, harbour scenes and marine objects were treated with a unique precision and fastidiousness.

The consequence of this general withdrawal from extreme manifestations of Cubism during the 1920s and 1930s, the abandonment of Surrealism and the temporary discarding of abstraction by all but a very few painters such as Ben Nicholson, meant that by 1939 the prevailing style of English painting was a gentle and refined romanticism.

War Artists deal in visual images. As far as possible they show what war looks like, rather that what it is about. They were required to record what they saw, 'to report on a landscape'. The best war paintings, nevertheless, whether they are imaginative reconstructions like the aerial battles of Paul Nash or on the spot records like the great convoy pieces by Richard Eurich, say something relevant about the nature of war and the feelings of those taking part.

Ruined landscapes and trench warfare were the main subjects of war painting between 1914–18: the combatants were often within sight of each other, and they were aware of the killed and wounded on both sides. In the

NEVINSON, C.R.W.,
*The Road from Arras to*
*Bapaume*, Oil, 24 × 18 ins

Second World War this was rarely the case. Battles on both sea and land were fought from a distance, bombers rarely stayed long enough overhead to calculate the effects of their bombs. This difference in perspective is easily observable in the art of the two periods. In the First World War the most memorable war pictures were painted by artists who had been or were still serving soldiers. They not only saw, but they had experienced.

This was not the case in the Second World War. Although three war artists were killed—Eric Ravilious, Albert Richards, Thomas Hennell—only Richards of these saw action as a soldier. For the most part war artists were a race apart, non-combatants. The older among them—Stanley Spencer, Henry Moore, Wyndham Lewis, Paul Nash, C.R.W. Nevinson,

EURICH, Richard, *The Great Convoy to North Africa*, 1942, Oil, $14\frac{1}{2} \times 50$ ins

John Nash—had served in one capacity or another during the First World War, mainly in France. A few others, Edward Ardizzone from the Army, Leonard Rosoman from the Fire Service, John Worsley from the Navy, were subsequently commissioned as war artists. By and large, though, the war artists with whom this book deals, worked in an official rather than a private capacity. There were exceptions—Keith Vaughan, William Scott, for example—but it remains a fact that most Second World War art was produced to order.

Also observable is the absence of any note of passionate protest in the art of the Second World War. The necessity of the war was so generally accepted, the horrors of war, from the art, literature and photographs of twenty-five years earlier, had become so familiar, that there was no need to emphasise them. The tone of much of the works reproduced in this book is almost laconic. What was new were the particular circumstances: the machines, the locations, the weapons. It could be said with some truth that the machines, not the men who used them, were the greater objects of curiosity. Radar and similar sophisticated equipment controlled tanks, ships, aircraft, guns, torpedoes and bombs, and if the men handling such equipment seemed sometimes of less significance it was hardly the fault of the artist. Except in such brief, if crucial, episodes as the Battle of Britain individual combat in anything like a gladiatorial or chivalrous manner was

a thing of the past.

Few war artists felt themselves required to express an attitude to the war, moral or otherwise. There was no need, the war was a fact not a political crusade. There is no propaganda in these pictures beyond the fact that they record successive stages of a necessary war — a war for survival — from near defeat to ultimate victory.

While few war-time posters were made by the painters mentioned in this book, a number of talented designers and cartoonists combined to put over urgent messages in poster form. Posters were no longer required, as in 1914–18, to shame volunteers into joining the Services, since conscription was in force, and it was only the women's Services that relied on recruiting campaigns. Nevertheless, in Britain — as also in France, America, Germany and Russia — campaigns were launched through posters on such subjects as careless talk, the need for economy, the value of drinking milk, the importance of saving, and so on.

Joseph Darracott, in his booklet *Second World War Posters*, emphasises the increase, during the Second World War, of government control. As the work of voluntary organisations and charities came to be replaced by government departments, so the need for individually produced posters declined. Typically, in Britain, it was cartoonists like Fougasse — *Careless Talk Costs Lives*, Bruce Bairnsfather — *Even the Walls ...*, and Bert Thomas

*Colours of War*

—*Is Your Journey Really Necessary?* who made the greatest impact and whose slogans have passed into the language. Abstract art, Cubism, and Surrealism all had influence on the design of recruiting posters, as did the Bauhaus on their typography.

The poetry of the Second World War was low-key; not a poetry of protest but one of acceptance and endurance. The compassion was in the sharing. This is true, too, of the art, dealing as it does in camaraderies of confinement, whether in barracks, aircraft, or mess-decks, as much as in scenes of devastation or military preparation.

For the painter, much more than for the writer, the *matériel* of war — armaments, equipment, gadgetry, machines, uniforms — is interesting for its own sake. Leonard Rosoman records later in this book his fascination with the relationship between men and machines in an aircraft carrier. Soldiers with their guns and their tanks, pilots with their aircraft, sailors with their ships — these all do enjoy a special relationship, in which dependence, trust and beauty play their part. The Futurist's excitement over the elegance of the machine was generated by its novelty, but it was perfectly possible for painters thirty years later to express an equivalent pleasure in the technical precision and design of agents of destruction.

ARMSTRONG, John, *Burnt-out Aeroplane*, Tempera, $11\frac{1}{2} \times 19$ ins

CARR, Henry, *A Camouflaged 25 Pounder Gun in action near Medjez-El-Bab*, Oil, 34 × 41 ins

In the memorable opening to *The Last Enemy*, when he describes landing in the sea after being shot down, Richard Hillary quotes four lines by Verlaine:

> Quoique sans patrie et sans roi,
> Et très brave ne l'étant guère,
> J'ai voulu mourir à la guerre
> La mort n'a pas voulu de moi

In the end, of course, death granted his wish. Of those three artist casualties of the war, Ravilious failed to return from a reconnaissance flight off Iceland, Richards was blown up by a mine during the Rhine offensive, Hennell disappeared in Indonesia. The bodies of none were recovered.

Of the poets of the war Sidney Keyes was taken prisoner in North Africa and died in enemy hands, Alun Lewis was killed in an accident by his own revolver on the Arakan front, Keith Douglas was killed in Normandy, Drummond Allison in action on the Garigliano. Their poems and their areas of service find apt illustration in the works of their painter colleagues.

Verlaine's first two lines have a curious relevance to war artists, whose country and king were essentially of the imagination, almost to the extent of making them dispassionate observers of conflict, rather than participants. Germany had its distinguished painters of the First World War—Otto Dix, who survived it, Macke and Marc, who did not—but after Hitler came to power German painters of repute were either dead or in exile.

The French began to paint the war only after it was over, the Italians had virtually no war art, and the Americans, unaccountably, employed mainly commercial artists. British war art, therefore, has to stand, neutrally in a sense, for both Allies and enemies.

For reasons I have suggested there were probably no individual paintings to come out of the Second World War that compare with the best work done by Paul Nash and Nevinson between 1914 and 1919, paintings such as Nash's *The Menin Road, After the Battle, We are Making a New World*, and Nevinson's *La Mitrailleuse* and *Returning to the Trenches*.

But if this should be so, then there was an altogether greater variety, of both subject and style, in the art produced between 1939 and 1945. For some painters the war was no more than an interruption to their real work. But for nearly all those featured in this book it was a deepening and significant experience, its effects discernible on all their subsequent work, not only on that with a war subject. This was as true of Moore and Sutherland as of anyone else.

The shelter sketches of Henry Moore, the paintings of bombed buildings by Graham Sutherland and John Piper are well enough known. But there were also, outstandingly, Spencer's shipbuilding panels, done at Port Glasgow on the Clyde; Ravilious's cool watercolours of ships and aircraft in northern waters; Rosoman's richly painted flight-deck pictures done in the Far East later in the war; Albert Richard's glider and bridge-demolition pictures done in the heat of battle during the Allied advance. These had no equivalent in the war art of 1914–18. And it was only Nash's own work in that war that created more haunting images than his *Totes Meer* painting of 1940–1, in which he envisaged a dump of shot-down German planes as a struggling sea of metal washed by moonlight, or than Richard Eurich's

LAMB, Henry, *A Command Post*, Oil, 24¾ × 54 ins

DRING, William, *Leading
Seaman A. Beale in the
Loading Chambers*, Pastel,
$18\frac{1}{2} \times 12\frac{1}{2}$ ins

*Great Convoy to North Africa, 1942* and his *Dunkirk Beaches*.

There was another side to war art, less immediate, more topographical, and touching at one time or another on Cairo. Edward Bawden, Anthony Gross, Edward Ardizzone, William Coldstream were among those who painted the desert war, and subsequently the Italian landings, though Bawden and Gross were to go much further afield. Coldstream confined himself largely to portraits, but the informal kind of diary paintings done by the others in the desert; Egypt and Arakan (Gross); the Sudan, Abyssinia, Libya, Syria and Iraq (Bawden); helped to build up a picture of British and Allied involvement that exceeded anything possible in the First World War. Gross and Bawden, in particular, travelled on a scale that even Edward Lear might have envied. A pre-war ruralist like Thomas Hennell, who would in all probability have rarely moved out of the English countryside, was enabled to send back pictures from Iceland, Normandy, Holland, Burma and Penang before disappearing into the blue.

In this way the war opened the eyes and extended the experience of a

ROSOMAN, Leonard, *A Sunken Ship in Hong Kong Harbour*, Watercolour, $15\frac{1}{2} \times 20\frac{1}{2}$ ins

whole generation of painters. A sense of waste and growing futility was what activated the most moving poetry and painting of the Great War, the feeling that the youngest and best were being needlessly sacrificed on the muddy fields of Flanders. There was little such reaction to the outbreak of war in 1939. All wars are wasteful and tragic, but if ever there seemed a war that had to be fought, whatever the consequences, it was the anti-Nazi war of 1939–45. The calm acceptance of that fact affected the tone of all its poetry and painting. Whatever the inconvenience, discomfort, boredom and danger of the war, whatever its casualties, no writer or artist seriously questioned its validity. What is more, it is plain from the work discussed and illustrated in this book that the challenge of accepting discipline, of working in a sense to order, produced remarkable and sometimes surprising results. This was no less the case with artists of such powerful and subjective vision as Sutherland and Moore as with those concerned with more familiar representations of reality.

BAWDEN, Edward, *Aid to Russia*, Watercolour, $15\frac{1}{2} \times 40\frac{1}{8}$ ins

GROSS, Anthony, *Sandbags in Bethnal Green*, 1940, Pen, ink and wash, $12\frac{1}{2} \times 20$ ins

# I ═══════════════════════════

# ART AND WAR
## *The War Artists' Advisory Committee*

He plays with death and animality;
And reading in the shadows of his pallid flesh I see
The idea of Michelangelo's cartoon
Of soldiers bathing, breaking off before they were half done
At some sortie of the enemy, an episode
Of the Pisan wars with Florence. I remember how he showed
Their muscular limbs that clamber from the water,
And heads that turn across the shoulder, eager for the slaughter,
Forgetful of their bodies that are bare,
And hot to buckle on and use the weapons lying there.
— And I think too of the theme another found
When, shadowing men's bodies on a sinister red ground,
Another Florentine, Pollaiuolo,
Painted a naked battle: warriors, straddled, hacked the foe,
Dug their bare toes into the ground and slew
The brother-naked man who lay between their feet and drew
His lips back from his teeth in a grimace.

They were Italians who knew war's sorrow and disgrace
And showed the thing suspended, stripped: a theme
Born out of the experience of war's horrible extreme
Beneath a sky where even the air flows
With lacrimae Christi ...

F.T. Prince, *Soldiers Bathing*

*Terms of Reference*

...to draw up a list of artists qualified to record the War at home and abroad. In co-operation with the Services Departments, and other Government Departments, as may be desirable, to advise on the selection of artists from this list for War purposes and on the arrangements for their employment. To advise on such questions as copyright, disposal, and exhibition of works and the publication of reproductions.

The War Artists' Advisory Committee, some of whose terms of reference appear at the head of this chapter, held its first meeting, under the chairmanship of Sir Kenneth Clark, at the National Gallery on November 23, 1939. There were to be 197 weekly meetings in all, the last of them held on December 28, 1945. The first meeting was attended by Sir Muirhead Bone, Sir Walter Russell, and P.H. Jowett, representing the arts; T.B. Braund represented the Home Office, W.P. Hildred, the Air Ministry, C.R. Coote, the War Office, and R.M.Y. Gleadowe, the Admiralty.

The constitution of the Committee remained roughly the same throughout the war, though from time to time departmental and service members changed and the occasional additional member was co-opted. At the start of its existence, and most influentially, the Secretary was E.M.O'R. Dickey of the Ministry of Information.

This book is in no sense a history of the official War Artists' scheme, but since it was virtually impossible for artists to operate outside it, some account of its doings is necessary. One or two painters did in fact produce imaginative 'war' pictures on their own initiative—William Scott, Ceri Richards and Edward Burra come to mind—but mostly those submitted to the Committee for purchase were of little account.

RAVILIOUS, Eric,
*Destroyers at Night*,
Watercolour,
$16\frac{3}{4} \times 22\frac{1}{2}$ ins

LOWRY, L.S.,
*Going to Work*, 1943, Oil,
18 × 24 ins

In the First World War artists had either been given honorary commissions, the Government acquiring what works of theirs they chose in return for their officers' salary, or else they received agreed fees for specific pieces of work. These alternative proposals were adhered to in the Second World War, the majority of artists coming into the second category.

The artists selected by the War Artists' Advisory Committee were, in a sense, a protected species. They were to do with the war, but not in it. Inevitably, they had, most of the time, to be behind the battle, though as the war progressed and the military authorities became more accustomed to the idea of the war artist as camp follower, painters came increasingly to share in the experiences of front-line troops. They flew, like Ravilious; went to sea like Worsley, Freedman, Rosoman and Hennell; parachuted, like Albert Richards. There was no escape from danger in such circumstances.

In the early stages of the war, war artists complained frequently about their distance from the action, their exclusion from proscribed or sensitive areas. Things gradually improved, especially once new fronts had been opened up. By the time the war had finished no phase of the fighting was left uncovered by war artists.

At the first meeting Sir Kenneth Clark, after various discussions about the scope of the Committee, the preparation of a list of artists and arrangements for their employment, summed up by confirming that the three Service departments would adopt a scheme providing for (1) a few full-time artists (2) specific commissions (3) permits for those who applied on their own initiative.

A Ministry of Labour Committee had already drawn up a provisional list of artists 'suitable for recording the War'. 'The War' was subsequently

replaced by 'wartime activities'. The amendment seems significant, because for some time there was little war to record and when there was few artists were allowed anywhere near it.

CARR, Henry, *Parachute Drop*, Oil, 30 × 40 ins

The first list contained over 50 names, most of them predictable: veterans of the First World War, eminent R.A.s, leading portrait painters, a sprinkling of women—Laura Knight, Vanessa Bell, Eve Kirk among them. Nearly all of them at one time or another were given commissions, though Bomberg not for some time and William Nicholson, Pasmore and Wadsworth not at all.

A number of subject categories were established, such as portraits, figures in action (front and home), landscape, sea and shipping, sky and aeroplanes, towns and factory exteriors, factory interiors and battleship equipment (technical requirements), and general. It was the task of the Committee to match subject and artist.

On November 29, 30 artists were considered and 23 recommended. *Strongly* recommended were Ardizzone, Freedman, Kennington and Medley; those recommended included Paul and John Nash, Nevinson, Lamb, Wyndham Lewis, Bawden and Coldstream.

MONNINGTON, W.,
*Fighter Affiliation*, Oil,
$18\frac{1}{4} \times 16\frac{1}{4}$ ins

Of Paul Nash it was remarked that he should be 'encouraged to tackle the sky and aeroplanes'. Medley was considered 'very suitable for the War Office'. The first proposals made by the Committee were that Kennington should do portraits of Lord Gort, General Ironside and other prominent service leaders, that William Roberts should draw heads of Other Ranks, and Henry Rushbury munition works.

The next meeting of the Committee *strongly* recommended Ravilious, Roberts and Rushbury, and recommended Pitchforth ('a rapid worker'), Piper, Wadsworth, Sutherland and the two Spencers.

The same meeting received a copy of a letter from the Treasury to the War Office, their Lordships sanctioning the appointment of 1 Portrait Painter, 1 General Painter, 1 Etcher, 1 black and white artist, each to be offered an honorary commission and an annual salary of £650.

On December 20, John Nash and Eric Ravilious were assigned to the Admiralty, Ardizzone, Freedman and Medley to the War Office, and Bawden and Paul Nash to the Air Ministry.

The fourteen bound volumes of the Committee's minutes make spasmodically interesting reading. There were occasional spats, when the Air Ministry representatives, for example, complained of inaccuracy in the work of Paul Nash and Richard Eurich, and of the rejection of Frank

Wootton, a more literal, if more limited, artist. In the ensuing correspondence artistic merit was supported against documentary realism.

For the most part, though, the Committee's deliberations were over routine matters: the control and dispersal of artists, the suggesting of subjects and selecting of pictures to purchase, the arranging of exhibitions, the vetting of new applications, questions of copyright, uniform, materials, fees, travel expenses, permits, clothing coupons.

Committee meetings tend to conform to predictable patterns. Some items taken more or less at random from the minutes and letters to and from the Secretary give an idea of what took place. They are necessarily fragmentary, and usually there is no record of follow-up.

20–12–39  Letters to be written to John and Sickert.
29–12–39  Letters to Robert Medley in A.R.P. offering 50 gns for 8 pictures of scenes at a disembarkation port in France and of 'life at the base'.
11–1–40  Medley refused permission to go to France by the War Office ('M.I.5?' is noted in the margin) and appointed to do Civil Defence.
11–1–40  Messrs Foggie, Hutchison and Wellington question the absence of Scottish artists.
13–1–40  W.P. Hildred, Air Ministry, in a letter to Mr. W.G. Nott-Bower, P.E.O. 'You will see from the file that the War

WILKINSON, Norman,
*Wellington Bombers attacked by German Fighters during an Offensive Reconnaissance over Wilhelmshaven,
18 December 1939*, Oil,
40 × 15 ins

Artists' Advisory Committee suggested to us Paul Nash and Edward Bawden. They are both a bit leftish and I myself dislike Bawden's work or what I saw of it. So does P.U.S., and in the result the War Office have snapped him up, and the A.I.A. Committee may be recommending Keith Henderson in his place, but I do not know. So far as Nash is concerned, he is, I think, acceptable, but he has ideas and wants to be paid as much as Sir Muirhead Bone. This I think is wrong ...'

7–2–40     John Nash and Eric Ravilious appointed Captain, Royal Marines. Medley authorised to travel third class.

7–2–40     122 artists considered, 96 rejected as unsuitable. Among six recommended, the names of David Low and Henry Moore. Put on Reserve list, Bomberg, Buhler, Lowry.

21–2–40     Memorandum from Dickey:
'Mr. Roberts called this morning and I explained to him that the Service representatives on the A/A committee were not prepared to allow him to undertake any more drawings of Service personalities and that the committee fully supported them ... Mr. Roberts was very angry at what he described as the high-handed attitude of the Service people ... He fully understood, however, that it is no use his making a fuss.'

HAILSTONE, Bernard, *Loading Ammunition at Hull Docks*, 1943, Oil, 25 × 30 ins

A note against Coldstream 'a slow worker'.

6–3–40 Dickey to Coote:
'Dear Coote,
There is a man called Richard Ellis who has been plaguing the life out of us here. His trouble is that he wants to be both an official artist and a spy at the same time ... I seem fated to refer to you people whose handwriting nobody can read.'

18–3–40 Sir Kenneth Clark reports to the Minister of Information that seven salaried posts have been filled, Sir Muirhead Bone (Admiralty), Ardizzone, Bawden, Eves and Freedman (War Office), Paul Nash and Keith Henderson (Air Ministry). John Nash, Eric Ravilious and Anthony Gross have been given specific commissions.

19–8–40 Dickey to Clark:
'Ardizzone's criticism that as non-commissioned (after having held a commission!) he was never allowed on real scene of ops—all he could draw were soldiers in parks and pubs ... I am sure that our present collection of pictures suffers from the presence of too many works which are easily criticised as remote from the actual war.'

BONE, Sir Muirhead,
*Lowering a Mine into the Mining Deck*, 1940, Pen, chalk and wash,
$14 \times 21\frac{3}{4}$ ins

In November 1940 an exhibition of war paintings was held at the Museum of Modern Art, New York. This contained work by Ardizzone, Bawden, Gross, Pitchforth, Ravilious and Sutherland.

22–12–40    Dickey writes to Clark (absent ill) about replacing Bone and Jowett, regular absentees from meetings. He puts forward reasons for not wanting a gallery man (e.g. Rothenstein from the Tate) because of possible conflict with Imperial War Museum and National Maritime Museum over ultimate disposal of pictures, and suggests the need for artists on the committee, John, perhaps, or from those already working Kennington 'though he might be troublesome and more bother than he would be worth…Paul Nash would be impossible, but Ardizzone would be good, I think his outlook is a catholic one.'

Clark replied that John could no longer be bothered and that he was against appointing artists already employed on grounds of apparent favouritism. He suggested Professor Randolph Schwabe of the Slade to replace Jowett. This was agreed.

16–1–41    Dickey to Clark, referring to Coote's fuss about Ardizzone's two drawings of Staff Officers at Wilton House among

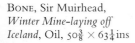

Bone, Sir Muirhead, *Winter Mine-laying off Iceland*, Oil, $50\frac{3}{8} \times 63\frac{1}{4}$ ins

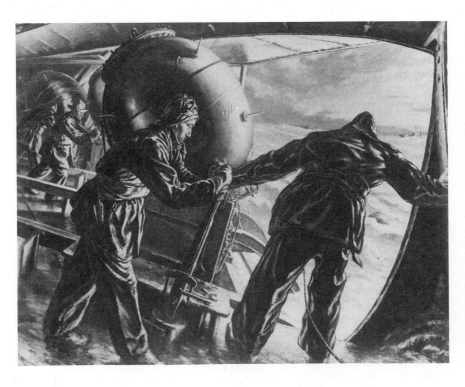

ROGERS, Claude,
*Sappers Wiring*, Oil,
21 × 27 ins

naked venuses and his wish for them to be removed from the
National Gallery in case of complaints, he writes that this has
been done.

30–7–41 Extract from minutes:
'Mr. Carel Weight's picture of a German aeroplane swoop-
ing down on a trolley bus was found unacceptable as not
fulfilling the conditions of his commission. Agreed that he be
asked to try again.'

6–8–41 Dickey to Clark (on the subject of Air Commodore Peake,
the Air Ministry representative, who had complained about
the rejection of the technically accurate aircraft paintings of
Frank Wootton. Clark had given him reasons and received in
reply a discursive letter):
'From my recollection of your letter to him of July 8 his to
you of the 31st does not constitute anything like a satisfactory
reply. Surely he might have been expected to take your
points one by one and deal with them as well as he could. I
always thought that *was* the way to answer a letter. Instead he
has ridden off on a vague generalisation about the need for
taking a "broad view" and suggests a conference at the Air
Ministry in order to arrive at a policy which will satisfy
"both points of view", by which I take him to mean the
point of view which puts faithful representation before artistic
merit and the point of view of your committee.'

19–11–41  The Chairman, who had written to Sir William Nicholson in accordance with the committee's recommendation that he be asked to consider painting a picture of a bombed building converted for water storage, reported that Sir William was unwilling to have subjects suggested for him.

The Ministry of Supply reported that Mr David Bomberg had approached them with a request to do publicity design for Russia. The artist had not been encouraged.

7–1–42  Eric Ravilious's request to be sent to R.A.F. wing in Russia: this was approved but found impossible to arrange.

4–2–42  Under the heading Dilatory Artists it was agreed that the Secretary write to the following whose pictures had not yet been delivered:

Robert Austin (Women manning a barrage balloon)
Kenneth Rowntree (C.E.M.A. Concert)
John Piper (Underground Aircraft Factory)

17–6–42  'Sir Muirhead Bone said that in compiling artistic records of the last war it had been the aim of those concerned to secure pictures of events and activities by those who had taken part in them or had been there to see for themselves. He felt that more should be done in the catalogues ... to make clear to the public whether a picture was by an eyewitness, such as Worsley's sinking *Laurentic*, a reconstruction, such as Cundall's *Dunkirk*, or an imaginary scene, such as Coxon's shipwrecked men on a raft.'

2–9–42  '16 gns to be paid to Keith Vaughan for 8 drawings of army life.'

PEARS, Charles, *A German Searchlight across the English Channel*, 1942, Oil, 32 × 50 ins

Eurich, Richard, *Night Attack over Southampton Water*, Oil, 14 × 24 ins

15–7–42   A.N. Palmer took over as Secretary to the Committee, Dickey returning to the Board of Education.

23–9–42   Palmer replaced by G. Elmslie Owen. At this meeting the death of Eric Ravilious on September 2 was announced and the question of compensation and a small outstanding mess bill discussed.

2–10–42   'To: The Director, Communications and General

From: Mr. Elmslie Owen

### Artists' Advisory Committee

This Committee meets weekly at the National Gallery. The principal business of the committee is

(a) To receive and discuss Departmental Reports.
(b) To review works submitted for purchase.
(c) To appoint artists from time to time to serve with the Department concerned, and to commission work as occasion arises.
(d) To discuss and, when necessary, revise, policy.
(e) To deal generally with exhibitions of War Artists' pictures, at home and overseas.

I suggest —
(a) that this Committee is necessary.
(b) that a weekly meeting is necessary.
(c) that no reduction of the number of members is possible.
(d) that the present procedure is satisfactory.
No additional Committee has been set up.'

4–11–42  'Mr. Paul Nash. Arrangements have been made for a night flight for this artist.'

30–12–42  'Mr Wyndham Lewis has written protesting that the fee offered for his commission is inadequate. He points out that in the last war he did two large pictures for £300. It was pointed out that there could be no comparison between the fee for a large picture and the fee for a set of drawings.'

6–1–43  'Captain Ardizzone has completed 12 drawings of the El Alamein battle, and is proceeding to the long-range Desert Groups.'
'Captain Gross should have left for India some weeks ago ... the Secretary was instructed to have sent to Captain Gross 50 sheets of paper.'

13–9–43  'Home Security: Mr Kenneth Rowntree. This artist has accepted the commission to paint jam-making, which is being done by the Women's Institute.'

Early in 1944 the Ministry of Information issued, under the heading Artists' Advisory Committee, an 'interim report for the 4th year of the war'. The following extract from the section on artists holding full-time salaried posts, gives some idea of the movement of artists over whom the Committee had control.

There have been several changes in the artists who are working full-time. Rodrigo Moynihan has replaced Edward Bawden for the War Office, Edward Bawden has departed for Irak and Iran, and Thomas Hennell to Iceland under the Ministry of Information. Two additional War Office Artists have been appointed; Henry Carr to the First Army in North Africa and William Coldstream as Portrait Artist in the Middle East. Edward Bawden had a number of escapes while War Office Artist; he was torpedoed and rescued, put into an internment camp at Casablanca, there was rescued by the Americans when they landed and returned to this country after a stay in America. His kit and some of his paintings were lost ... We regret to announce the loss of Eric Ravilious who was reported missing since Sept 2, 1942, when the aircraft in which he was a passenger failed to return from patrol and he was subsequently reported officially killed ...

30–3–44  From letter to Coote at the War Office, recommending Ardizzone's transfer to the Admiralty:

'In view of the fact that there are no examples of this artist's work depicting naval subjects, it was agreed that it be recommended to the War Office that he be loaned to the Admiralty for 2 months to make pictures of the pre-invasion naval preparations ... To take but one example, it would be most unfortunate if, at the end of the war, it were found impossible to allot any of Captain Ardizzone's works to the National Maritime and other naval museums.'

McGRATH, Raymond, *Rear Turrets of a Whitley Aircraft*, 1940, Watercolour, $22\frac{3}{4} \times 29\frac{1}{8}$ ins

29–8–45   From minutes of 188th meeting:
'Leonard Rosoman has been on at least one and possibly two air strikes in the Pacific, attached to *H.M.S. Formidable*. A signal has been sent to him suggesting he tries to paint devastation and surrender scenes in Japan.'

Four months later the Committee, as originally constituted, held its last meeting.

# II

# THE RECEIVING END

*Henry Moore, Graham Sutherland,
John Piper*

Black leaves are piled against the roaring weir;
Dark closes round the manor and the hut;
The dead Knight moulders on his rotting bier.
And one by one the warped old casements shut
Alun Lewis, *Autumn 1939*

No less important was his willingness to refrain from imposing his own artistic personality on his material, in other words to refrain from turning every picture into an immediately recognizable Sutherland ... In this respect there is an obvious contrast between the war 'records' of Sutherland and those of Henry Moore. Why do Moore's drawings of miners or of people in air-raid shelters lack the feeling of reality, the human element, which comes across so strongly in Sutherland's pictures? The answer would seem to be that Moore, unlike Sutherland, chose to play down the factual aspects and human implications of a scene in order to extract something that was art for art's sake. Stylistically, Moore projects his own personality first and treats the cowering and sleeping crowds in shelters as models from whom he abstracts ideas for new sculptures.

Douglas Cooper, *The Work of Graham Sutherland*

In the shelter drawings he created a world peopled by figures at once monumental and ghostly. The colours that faintly illuminate this noble yet nightmare world are charged as deeply as the forms with the artist's intense emotion and they both explain and entrance them. In all he filled two sketchbooks and made about a hundred large drawings: standing, seated or reclining figures hieratic and immobile yet subtly expressive of Moore's humanity, encompassed by vast shadowy spaces brought to a vibrant life by the depths and brilliances of his colour ... These two small books—reservoirs of concentrated imaginative power—have to my thinking a place among Moore's most moving works.

John Rothenstein: *Modern English Painters*

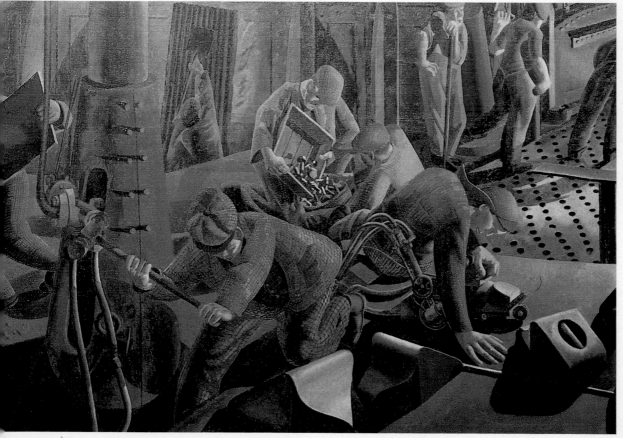

# Henry Moore

At the outbreak of war Henry Moore was teaching two days a week at Chelsea School of Art. The Art School was attached to the Polytechnic at Chelsea and both Henry Moore and Graham Sutherland volunteered to take the recently instituted precision tool-making course. They were told to be ready to start almost immediately. However, nothing materialised. Moore and his wife took over 7, Mall Studios in Hampstead from Ben Nicholson and Barbara Hepworth, who had left for Cornwall with their children, and Moore, unable to envisage the completion of any work of sculpture, occupied himself with drawing. 'Drawing keeps one fit,' he remarked to Herbert Read, 'like physical exercises — perhaps acts like water to a plant — and it lessens the danger of repeating oneself and getting into a formula.'

The Battle of Britain ended the hot summer of 1940; before long the German bombers were beginning their regular pounding of London and other cities. Henry Moore has himself described the chance experience that led to his shelter sketches:

> One evening after dinner in a restaurant with some friends we returned home by Underground taking the Northern Line to Belsize Park ... For the first time that evening I saw people lying on the platforms at all the stations we stopped at. When we got to Belsize Park we weren't allowed out of the station for an hour because of the bombing. I spent the time looking at the rows of people sleeping on the platforms. I had never seen so many reclining figures and even the train tunnels seemed to be like the holes in my sculpture. And amid the grim tension, I noticed groups of strangers formed together in intimate groups and children asleep within feet of the passing trains.
>
> After that evening I travelled all over London by Underground ... I never made any sketches in the Underground. It would have been like drawing in the hold of a slave ship. I would wander about sometimes passing a particular group that interested me half a dozen times. Sometimes, in a corner where I could not be seen, I would make notes on the back of an envelope.

In an interview with James Johnson Sweeney, published in *Partisan Review* in 1947 and quoted by Rothenstein in *Modern English Painters*, Moore remarked:

> The war from being an awful worry became a real experience. Quite against what I expected I found myself strangely excited by the bombed buildings, but more still by the unbelievable scenes and life of the underground shelters ... It was not until the Blitz in London that I began to realize how deep-rooted the Italian influence had been ... Here, curiously enough, is where, in looking back, my Italian trip and the

*opposite,*
PIPER, John, *The Passage to the Control-Room at S. W. Regional Headquarters, Bristol,* Oil, 30 × 20 ins

*overleaf above,*
RAVILIOUS, Eric, *Walrus Aircraft on the Slipway,* Watercolour, 19 × 21½ ins

MOORE, Henry,
*Shelter Scene: Bunks and
Sleepers*, Wash and
crayon, $18\frac{1}{4} \times 16\frac{1}{2}$ ins

Mediterranean tradition came once more to the surface. There was no discarding of those other interests in archaic art and the art of primitive peoples, but rather a clearer tension between this approach and the humanist emphasis.

In February 1917 Moore, aged 19, had joined the 15th London Regiment. He went to France, was gassed in the battle of Cambrai and invalided home. He ended the war a bayonet instructor at Aldershot, with the rank of Corporal.

When early in 1940 Sir Kenneth Clark invited Moore to become an official war artist he declined. However, Clark saw his shelter drawings and recommended to the War Artists' Advisory Committee that they be purchased. Accordingly, on January 2, 1941, Dickey, the Secretary of the Committee, wrote to Moore at Much Hadham (his Hampstead studio having been hit by a bomb) offering him 32 guineas for 4 drawings. In the same letter he offered Moore a commission to carry out 'a series of drawings of Civil Defence subjects' for 50 guineas. The letter ends 'with my best wishes to you and yours for a Happy New Year and the destruction of the Axis.' Moore accepted. 'I used to go to London two days a week spending the nights in the Underground and coming up at dawn.'

Moore's practice was to show the Committee 'eight or ten' drawings at a time. They would choose four or five, leaving him to dispose of the rest.

Moore's feelings of excitement about the Underground society of his first drawings faded when the authorities began to equip the shelters with bunks, canteens and washing facilities. 'With them the drama and the strangeness of the early months in the Underground began to recede both for me and for the people themselves.'

It was suggested therefore that Moore, who came of mining stock, return to Castleford, his birthplace, 'as a small boy these slag heaps seemed much larger than the Pyramids', to make drawings of miners at work. He went down a mine for the first time, and after two weeks sketching underground acquired enough material for three months of drawing. When he had completed this commission Moore intimated that he wanted to be left free to do his own work. Although the influence of his war drawings could be observed on many of his future sculptures, especially such large works as the three Battersea Standing Figures — 'I made them look into the distance, as if they were expecting something dramatic to happen. Drama can be implied without the appearance of physical action' — Moore undertook no further tasks specifically to do with war. His next commission was the Madonna and Child for St Matthew's Church, Northampton.

Although there may be differing views about the quality of Moore's shelter drawings, opinion is consistent that the mining experience failed, for some reason, to stimulate Moore. 'The shelter drawings came right after first being moved by the experience of them, whereas the coalmine drawings were more like a commission.'

For many war artists the element of 'commission' — of having strange subjects provided for them — was unexpectedly rewarding, bringing out qualities and responses in themselves that might otherwise have remained dormant. It seems, in this instance, not to have been the case for Moore. The mining expedition was 'two weeks physical sweat seeing the subject, and that number of months mental sweat trying to be satisfied carrying them out.'

Moore remarked in a conversation with Donald Hall, the author of a book on his work, *Henry Moore*, that going down the mines 'made clear many things about my own childhood' but that was as far as it went. Hall observes that 'the miners did not enter Moore's imagination and emerge transformed, the way the sleepers did. His drawings of coal miners hacking at the pit face are good pictures, with a muscular human energy to them, but they mean no more than what they represent.'

It was precisely the 'transforming' quality of Moore's shelter drawings, their stylisation of ordinary people into unmistakable studies for Moore sculptures, compared with Sutherland's subordination of personality to subject matter, that Douglas Cooper found distasteful.

It depends, of course, on whether one is considering Moore's 'war' drawings on their own terms or in relation to some specific function. The drawings of miners, bodies bent and glistening, their headlamps gleaming in darkness as they tunnelled, probed and hacked, convey, quite literally, endurance, resolution and purpose: Moore's notes on the margin of his sketches draw attention to 'whiteness' of lips, 'brilliant whites of eyes, cheekbones whiter than rest — most black round nose and creases from nose etc.'

Moore has himself described his procedure: 'I sketched with pen and ink, wax crayons and watercolour, using the wax-resist technique which I had discovered by accident before the war. I had been doing a drawing for my three-year-old niece using two or three wax crayons. Wishing to add some more colour, I found a box of watercolour paints and was delighted to see the watercolour run off the parts of the drawing that had a surface of wax. It was like magic and I found it very useful when doing my sketch books.'

Moore may have felt the limitations, in terms of sculpture, of these records of miners at work, but in many ways they are more sympathetic than the shelter drawings. Cooper is right in commenting on the lack of 'reality', of a 'human element' in the latter. It is not surprising that Moore recognised in the sleeping denizens of the Underground, with the black mouths of tunnels beyond them, and trains roaring past their heads, 'reclining figures' and 'the holes in my sculpture'. But they are not real people with lives outside the platform and recognisable feelings. The shelter forms seem either dead or not fully born; many of them, mere scatters of bones, seem to pre-figure Belsen. What Moore catches is the intimacy, bodies joined together under the flowing waves of blankets, the linking of arms. You can sense the foetidness of the atmosphere, the airlessness.

These shelter drawings had their admirers. In an article published in *Penguin New Writing* Keith Vaughan, refuting charges of morbidity and unreality, described them persuasively:

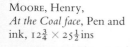

MOORE, Henry,
*At the Coal face*, Pen and
ink, $12\frac{3}{4} \times 25\frac{1}{2}$ ins

The qualities they stress are not less real because they lie deeper than the obvious and the apparent. Beside their more sculptural quality there is much that is simply human. Look at the two figures in *Green and Red Sleepers*, how a lifting fold of drapery lies like a caress across their shoulders, linking them together. The delicate and detailed modelling of lips and nostrils in the upturned faces seems to suggest the close-up minuteness and vividness of things in a dream, a troubled uncertain sleep; the smooth rounded contours broken into suddenly by the rake-like fingers of a hand clutching the blanket.

DOBSON, Frank, *The Flask: Arc-Welding Marine Boilers, Clydeside*, Pastel, $19\frac{7}{8} \times 30\frac{3}{4}$ ins

Vaughan found these drawings 'very moving' because Moore had not 'withheld himself from the full impact of this strange and tragic situation, but going beyond the apparent, has tried to discover and express those human and enduring qualities which would ultimately triumph and vindicate it.'

But, though their 'humanity' is apparent, they do not seem to me, despite Vaughan's advocacy, 'moving'. One is struck by a situation, a predicament, not by individual suffering. What Moore's figures express vividly is passivity, vulnerability, a shared context. It is possible to agree with Rothenstein's description of Moore's technical skill in these drawings, even his assessment of their power and beauty, and at the same time remain unmoved by them.

# Graham Sutherland

Now, looking as useless and as beautiful
As dragonflies, the plump silver balloons
Hang over London also like zany moons.

Yet from the blacked-out window death still seems
Private, not an affair that's shared by all
The distant people, the flats, the Town Hall.

Bernard Gutteridge, *In September 1939*

Graham Sutherland, like Henry Moore, had been teaching at Chelsea at the outbreak of war. When the school closed Sutherland moved to Tetbury in Gloucestershire and it was here, on June 6, 1940, that the Secretary of the War Artists' Advisory Committee wrote to Sutherland asking him to get in touch.

Five days later Dickey was reporting to Sturch at the Ministry of Supply that Sutherland had called and would gladly take on the transport of armaments by rail as a subject, though he would have preferred big gun foundries.

A month later Sutherland wrote to the Committee that he was sending up three gouaches, one of camouflaged bombers at dawn, and two of picketed aircraft. He was offered and accepted a fee of fifteen guineas.

From this time until 1945 Sutherland was in more or less continual employment, usually on six-month commissions, as an official war artist. He produced well over a hundred and fifty works of one kind or another, sketches, drawings, gouaches, though few oils.

SUTHERLAND, Graham,
*Camouflaged Bombers*,
1940, Oil, 18 × 27½ ins

SUTHERLAND, Graham,
*Devastation 1941: East End,*
*Burnt Paper Warehouse,*
Oil and watercolour
drawing, $26\frac{1}{2} \times 44\frac{3}{4}$ ins

Apart from one or two early pictures of aircraft—'I couldn't make much of them, I'm afraid'—Sutherland's war pictures fall into five main categories: bomb damage in South Wales and London; tin mines in Cornwall; steel works in Cardiff and Swansea; open-cast coal workings; and, finally, V.2 rocket sites and railway yards bombed by the R.A.F. in France.

Despite their evident differences the initial experiences of Moore and Sutherland were not dissimilar. Both experienced the Blitz, wandering among ruined streets after attacks, and both went underground. Sutherland has written as articulately as Moore about what he felt at the time and about how he went to work.

To begin with, South Wales: 'Swansea was the first sight I had of the possibilities of destruction as a subject. The architecture was florid and Victorian. At first I made as complete a record as I could of what I saw. I hadn't yet begun to feel any sense of what these remains really *looked* like. Later, some were to become like great animals who had been hurt.'

Next London:

> I will never forget those extraordinary first encounters: the silence, the absolute dead silence, except every now and again a thin tinkle of falling glass—a noise which reminded me of the music of Debussy.
>
> The first place I went to was the big area just north of St Paul's—I suppose about five acres—which had been almost completely flattened ...Sometimes fires were still burning. Everywhere there was a terrible stench—perhaps of burnt dirt; and always the silence ...Very occasionally there would be the crash of a building collapsing of its own volition. I would start to make perfunctory drawings here and there; gradually it was borne on me amid all this destruction how singularly one shape would impinge on another. A lift-shaft, for instance, the only thing left from what had obviously been a very tall building: in the way it had

fallen it was like a wounded animal. It wasn't that these forms *looked* like animals, but their movements were animal movements. One shaft in particular, with a very strong lateral fall, suggested a wounded tiger in a painting by Delacroix.

The two main areas in London where Sutherland worked were the East End, 'long terraces of houses remained: they were great—surprisingly wide—perspectives of destruction seeming to recede into infinity and the windowless blocks were like sightless eyes', and around St Paul's. 'Once I went on the roof of St. Paul's. The gathering place of authorities and others was the gallery round the base of the dome. This passage between walls was probably the strangest place in the cathedral. All, when not on duty, slept and lolled on deck-chairs. I remember thinking that it was like being on an ocean-liner.'

When the raids began to subside it was suggested to Sutherland that he go down to Cornwall where the tin mines had all been re-opened. It was a commission much like the Castleford mines had been for Moore. But Sutherland accepted it in quite a different way. 'To make drawings of the mines had only the vaguest relation to the war but I was certainly presented with a new world—and a world of such beauty and such mystery that I shall never forget it.'

Sutherland, who had, in his engineering days, been trapped for hours in a locomotive boiler, was afraid he would suffer from claustrophobia. But he accustomed himself to the darkness and the depth and during these months of 1942 produced some of his most beautiful drawings.

He has described how he did a number of portraits of miners to distract them from what he was really drawing. 'The heads I did were small and naturalistic, as suited their purpose; but the deeper significance of these men only gradually became clear to me. It was as if they were a kind of different

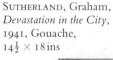

SUTHERLAND, Graham, *Devastation in the City*, 1941, Gouache, $14\frac{1}{2} \times 18$ ins

species—enobled underground, and with an added stature which above ground they lacked, and my feeling was that in spite of the hardness of the work in this nether world, this place held for them—subconsciously perhaps—an element of daily enthralment.'

It is impossible to imagine the more phlegmatic Moore, brought up among miners, reacting as freshly.

Sutherland has described the tunnel-life in words almost as vivid as his drawings: 'one would come across a miner sitting in a niche in a wall—like a statue, immobile ... the walls dripped water and the only light normally was from the acetylene lamps fixed to each man's helmet. Even today the smell of acetylene transports me immediately to the mine.'

In the autumn of 1942 Sutherland moved from Cornwall to Cardiff, to the steel works.

> The conception of the idea of stress, both physical and mental, and how forms can be modified by emotion, had been, even before the war, much in my mind. It was crystallised and strengthened by my understanding of Picasso's studies for *Guernica*. Faces become distorted by tears and mouths open in fear. Even a hand supporting a head creates distortion, as does the placing of food in the mouth.

SUTHERLAND, Graham, *Seated Miner Waiting*, Watercolour, $20\frac{1}{2} \times 14$ ins

I had seen aspects of this idea in certain kinds of destruction. So did I, too, in the steel works. As the hand feeds the mouth so did the long scoops which plunged into the furnace openings feed them, and the metal containers pouring molten iron into ladles had great encrusted mouths.

The acid green of moulds in iron foundries, the orange and pink of furnace flames, the ochre outcast coal and limestone quarries all bore recognisable affinities to the mainly Welsh landscapes Sutherland was painting before the war. The difference was mainly that in these war drawings the land was being vitally used, its deposits churned and transformed for industrial purposes. The Welsh landscapes are serene, however twisted the tree forms in them. In the drawings of 1942–3 men are thrust into the centre of proceedings, bearing the weight of the earth, at the fire's core. Like Moore, only more intensely, Sutherland was able to discover in unfamiliar sur-roundings familiar elements.

In late November 1944, Sutherland was sent to France. Astonishingly, it was the first time he'd ever been abroad. Paris had only recently been liberated and Sutherland's brief was to record what the flying-bomb sites, unphotographed even by the R.A.F., looked like.

He had a frustrating time getting to the sites at St Leu d'Esserent, whose whereabouts nobody seemed to know, and the marshalling yards at Trappes, but once there he made a series of gouaches that forcefully convey the devastation and dislocation — engines standing on end or on their sides, boilers and pistons in strange conjunctions, humps of earth heaved up as if by giant moles.

'I've never seen such a panoramic piece of devastation in my life,' he wrote, 'for miles the bridges and remnants of houses on either side of the river were like black spokes. A lot of Germans had been killed inside the caves and there was a terrible sweet smell of death in them.'

These 1944 gouaches were Sutherland's last works as a war artist. After it was all over he wrote revealingly about what the war meant to him as an artist and about war and art in general.

> Looking back on it, undoubtedly the war had an important effect on my consciousness. I never saw the concentration camps; I should in some ways have liked to have seen them. I remember receiving a black-covered American Central Office of Information book dealing with the camps. It was a kind of funeral book. In it were the most terrible photographs of Belsen, Auschwitz and Buchenwald … The whole idea of the depiction of Christ crucified became much more real to me after having seen this book and it seemed to be possible to do this subject again.

He raises the question as to how he might have coped with military or naval assignments. 'I feel sure that my thinking would not have been aroused by fighting on a grand scale entailing all the speed and mechan-

St Leu d'Esserent

SUTHERLAND, Graham,
*A Flying-Bomb Depot*,
Gouache, $11\frac{1}{2} \times 18\frac{3}{8}$ ins

isation of modern warfare; though no doubt individual battles, streets, and house fighting, might well have been another matter.'

It is interesting to compare Sutherland's modest disclaimers with Nevinson's statements after the Armistice in 1919, 'Artists were in love with the glory of violence…and when war came it found the modern artist equipped with a technique perfectly well able to express war.' Commenting on this, John Rothenstein, in his shrewd essay on Nevinson, observes, 'Futurism awakened them to a charmed acceptance of the beauties of the age of machines, but it did not equip them with a method of representing mechanized power … Their simultaneous representation of the successive stages of movements deprived them of the clarity which is an essential constituent of power.' It was Cubism, in Rothenstein's view, that provided Nevinson with a kind of 'magnificent shorthand perfectly adapted to convey the simplified essence of a mechanised apocalypse'.

Sutherland continues,

> But if the trappings in battle pictures—the uniforms, types of guns and the rest—are unsympathetic to me, this may well be because the effect of seeing bad descriptive work is stronger than one thinks: great battle pieces have been done which utilise the same material…but this material was always *recreated* and represented. And while it is true that at the root of my work is memory, plus the sudden unaccountable emotion which modifies and transforms facts, none the less these facts—these objective vocabularies—are invariably for me the necessary starting point. And in the particular context of modern warfare it is more than likely that I would have found these facts difficult or impossible to gather.

SUTHERLAND, Graham, *The City, A fallen lift shaft*, Gouache, $25\frac{1}{2} \times 44$ ins

In the course of his comments on Sutherland's war drawings Douglas Cooper accurately notes:

> Human beings appear rarely in these pictures, but when they do, as in the studies of steel workers and miners, they have the anxious and tense look of creatures in thrall to some monster ... there is in all Sutherland's paintings and drawings of the war an intense awareness of man and his activities. These gutted buildings and contorted girders, these blast-furnaces and desperate diggings, which make up the artist's personal imagery of the wartime scene, all signify immediately that they are man's handiwork. They may be grim and terrifying outward mani-festations of his passage, but everywhere we feel — even in his absence — the presence of man.

It is, I think, a fact that when the human figures first began to appear in Sutherland's war drawings it was often curiously anonymous and uncon-vincing — a concession to credibility, more than anything. The feeling had gone into inanimate objects. Later, the tin miners and iron workers, the latter usually faceless, bore in their professional anonymity the real burden of Sutherland's concern. The miners, in particular, as Edward Sackville-West described them, 'helmeted and crested with an acetylene flame, look as if they were made of the ore they are engaged in extracting ... their faces and hands are expressed in lines as taut and nervous as Dürer's'.

Roberto Tassi, the Italian critic, in his book, *Sutherland: the wartime drawings*, observes, 'In Sutherland, our atmosphere and a common scale link together the machinery, the flames, the people and the underground passages; the form reaches a peak of tension, a quintessence in which everything is concentrated and expressed.'

It is possible to regret that both Moore and Sutherland, for one reason or another, were obliged to be so far behind the battle, that they recorded what it was like always being on the receiving end. Moore had enough disagreeable experience in the first war, and both, as artists, had evolved sufficiently to have arrived at mature and identifying styles. But Sutherland in particular proved that he was adaptable and that he could make use of new experiences and subjects without losing his individuality. In a letter to Julian Andrews he described his war works as 'a kind of imaginative-realist journalism which in the nature of things had to be done rapidly and without long pondering and reflection.' Sutherland's habit was to make notes and drawings on the spot, and then work them up, through what he called a 'work-out' stage, into the more elaborate and detailed final product.

But if they are a kind of journalism Sutherland's drawings show a virtuosity and range that manage both to be suggestive as records and to work in terms of his own art. The jagged forms of broken machinery and falling brick, the searing colour of furnaces and foundries, the hollowed-out gloom of tunnels, all relate to — and act as a stage between — his works before and after the war. Aware of his own limitations, he was probably right in feeling that the action between armies and navies, the individual combat that flying involved, was not one to which his art was attuned. It is impossible, for example, to imagine Sutherland painting an imaginative war painting on any scale — in the manner, say, of Paul Nash. But what he did was to bring an immediacy and vividness of observation to brutal and profoundly felt experiences, and his notatory method recorded, with often haunting accuracy, the effects of bombing and the ways in which back-up weapons of war were forged.

DOBSON, Frank, *Bristol, November 24, 1940,* Watercolour, $22 \times 29\frac{1}{2}$ ins

# John Piper

They say that women, in a bombing raid,
Retire to sleep in brand new underwear
Lest they be tumbled out of doors, displayed
In shabby garments to the public stare.

You've often seen a house, sliced like a cheese,
Displaying its poor secrets—peeling walls
And warping cupboards. Of such tragedies
It is the petty scale that most appals.

Norman Cameron, *Punishment Enough*

John Piper, like Sutherland, was appointed a war artist in 1940. Not surprisingly, since so much of his painting had architectural subjects, he was sent to such places as Bristol, Bath and Coventry to paint the damage done to buildings by air-raids. During the late 1930s Piper had turned from painting highly personalised abstracts, and involvement with the abstract magazine *Axis*, edited by his wife and which closed in 1937, to what Sir John Betjeman has called 'abstract versions of English landscapes—Gothic façades giving on to distances, rocks and waterfalls conceived in coloured planes. The use of yellow was noticeable after the restrained greys and blues of the abstracts.'

These tentative gestures back to representation were reinforced by country journeys made all over England and Wales, the results of which were hundreds of impressionistic and romantic watercolours reflecting various aspects of ecclesiastical architecture and village landscape. The mood of these watercolours was often oppressive, largely due to the weather in Piper's skies. Betjeman, however, points out that Piper's skies were painted black not to indicate storm but to emphasise the colour of stone.

Piper has always been a theatrical painter, his vantage point chosen to provide the greatest dramatic effect. His war paintings, as a consequence, resemble stage sets or backcloths to ballets to an extent that it is sometimes difficult to associate them with real events. Yet he had often visited the places he painted when, as he wrote to the Tate, 'the ruins were still smouldering and bodies were being dug out.'

Some of his earlier commissions, such as those for A.R.P. Posts or the Control Room at South West Regional Headquarters, Bristol, were not regarded either by himself or by others as particularly successful; yet the schematic detachment and dry precision of the Control Room oils convey much the same sort of atmosphere as some of the 1930s' abstracts. The bomb pictures, such as Lansdowne Chapel, Bath, and All Saints, Knowle, Bristol are unmistakable Pipers in their architectural detail and colouring, yet a sense of loss on any personal scale is missing. These churches, gutted and with rubble strewn around altars open to sky, have backdrop thinness.

They seem not to be places of human congregation or devotion; the insult to them is essentially aesthetic.

The Bath and Bristol pictures are painted with the charm and fluency, much freer in brushstrokes than his pre-war work, that came to characterise the many gouaches and watercolours Piper did in the 1960s, mainly in France and Italy. They are 'war' pictures, deterrent in impact, only in the most marginal sense, for all the vandalism of their subject matter. Yet the watercolours, if rarely the large oils, manage to bring together many of Piper's best qualities, what Medley, in a *Penguin New Writing* article, describes as the romantic view but 'equipped with the disciplines of an abstract painter ... His eye notes the proportions of the confronting masonry, translates them to terms of abstract relationships, dramatises them with colour, then comes to the texture; the scrubbed areas, the scratched, the glazed colour, the built-up impasto, the areas glow like stained glass locked in a framework of black.'

Piper, strangely enough, seems to me more persuasive in works that have little connection with the kind of subjects he might, left to himself, have chosen: American locomotives awaiting shipment, corvettes under construction. The backgrounds of low hills outside Cardiff, the terraced houses on a bluff above Bristol, bear authentic Piper mannerisms, but the engine and corvette have a detailed finish and cleanness of outline that make them solid presences. They are imaginative—realist journalism altogether more realist than anything Sutherland ever produced.

It may be that, in the general context of Piper's work, these various set

PIPER, John,
*Repairs and Repainting
Warships returned from
the beaches: Bristol,*
Watercolour,
$20\frac{7}{8} \times 26\frac{3}{8}$ ins

PIPER, John, *American Locomotives awaiting trans-shipment on the foreshore of Cardiff*, Watercolour, $21\frac{1}{4} \times 26\frac{1}{2}$ ins

subjects for the War Office and the Ministry of Information will seem to have less authenticity and relevance than the paintings of falling masonry, but they are evidence of a disciplined attention proper to their purpose.

In his book *British Romantic Artists* Piper wrote, 'Abiding also in the romantic painting of this country is the sense of drama in atmosphere, in the weather and the seasons. As a race we have always been conscious of the soft atmosphere and the changeable climate ...' Piper's own sense of drama resulted perhaps in a superfluously heightened atmosphere, a theatricality that war itself provided. In the meticulous, lower-key paintings the machinery of war speaks for itself.

# III

# VETERANS

*Stanley Spencer, Wyndham Lewis,
David Bomberg, John Nash, William Roberts,
Henry Lamb*

## Stanley Spencer

    These dry themselves and dress,
Combing their hair, forget the fear and shame of nakedness.
Because to love is frightening we prefer
The freedom of our crimes. Yet, as I drink the dusky air,
I feel a strange delight that fills me full,
Strange gratitude, as if evil itself were beautiful,
And kiss the wound in thought, while in the west
I watch a streak of red that might have issued from Christ's breast.

F.T. Prince, Soldiers Bathing

Stanley Spencer was one of only half-a-dozen or so war artists of quality—Paul Nash, John Nash, C.R.W. Nevinson, William Roberts and Henry Lamb were probably the most considerable of the others—who saw service of one kind or another in both World Wars. Spencer, though the Ministry of Information had requested that he be made a war artist in 1918, when he was serving in Macedonia, had been unable to get permission from his regiment. In consequence, it was only after he had been invalided home, in 1919, that he was able to start work on any commission. The result was his large and serenely compassionate painting *Travoys with Wounded Soldiers* and the various associated sketches, most of them fairly small, done at the same time—*Making a Red Cross, Scrubbing Clothes, Wounded being carried by Mules*. Spencer's Macedonian pictures, commissions though they were, and painted far from their subjects, convey, in his simple, idiosyncratic way, a real sense of comradeship and shared suffering. The most humdrum of army activities are given a ritualistic significance, and though Spencer suddenly lost his feeling for the Balkans and was anxious to shed involvement with war themes it was predictable that he would return to them. This he did, and by the summer of 1924 he was hard at work on compositions based on both his period as a medical orderly at Beaufort Hospital, Bristol and his service in Macedonia. These drawings, nearly all of them devoted to routine activities rather than military action, formed the basis of the wall paintings for Burghclere Chapel in Berkshire which occupied Spencer from 1927 to 1931. Culminating in *Resurrection of the Soldiers* the Burghclere pictures form the most profoundly felt and complete account of soldiering ever produced by a British painter.

The outbreak of war in 1939 found Spencer in severe financial straits, deprived of any market for the landscapes off which he had reluctantly lived for years. In January 1940, however, after an interview with Dickey of the War Artists' Advisory Committee, Spencer suggested a Crucifixion deriving from the occupation of Poland. In line with the general policy of getting artists only to paint what they saw, this idea was turned down. Instead, it was agreed that Spencer should record the activities of a shipyard; accordingly, he set off in May for Lithgow's shipyards in Port Glasgow.

Spencer's involvement with Port Glasgow lasted throughout the 1940s. His commissioned paintings *Shipbuilding on the Clyde* occupied him until the end of the war. Even before he had finished these — and by 1945 he had, not surprisingly, lost most of his initial enthusiasm — he had conceived the idea of painting a series of Resurrection pictures based on Port Glasgow.

Spencer, from his arrival in Port Glasgow until he left it, kept in constant touch with both the War Artists' Advisory Committee and his friends, and his notes and letters of the time give a detailed account of how he set about his task.

He was fortunate in that, as in Macedonia, the routine and atmosphere related to experiences in his own life; his childhood, his time as a medical orderly, his years as a private soldier. He was moved by the feeling of community in the dockyard, the dependence of one worker on another.

SPENCER, Stanley,
*Shipbuilding on the Clyde:*
*Bending the Keel Plate*,
Oil, 30 × 228 ins

Spencer worked quickly and after immediate approval of his pre-liminary sketches and first painting, *Burners*, he set to work on completing a polyptych. *Burners* was followed by further canvases on such activities as welding, riveting, rigging, bending keel plates, plumbing and caulking.

Spencer made frequent visits to Port Glasgow but most of the actual painting was done at the White Hart Inn, Leonard Stanley (*Burners*), Epsom and Cookham.

The series, despite Spencer's gradual switching of interest from ship-building to his resurrection project, was undoubtedly a success. 'Every-thing I see is manifestly religious and sexual,' Spencer wrote, describing his visit to a rigger's loft, and his reverence for the skill of the various workers. The 'respect and peace' which contemplation of their hard work and endurance produced in him gave his tightly organised panels a sense of sublimity and spiritual fervour, as well as of humming activity. *Burners*, especially, has remarkable spaciousness and warmth, the more remarkable considering how much Spencer was able to get into an enclosed, claustro-phobic area, with so many disparate but interdependent tasks going on. None of the later panels has quite the same forcefulness and glow as *Burners*, which was not only the first to be painted but the quickest to be finished. Most critics have called attention to the increasingly perfunctory, cramped and unfocused nature of the series, but if formal preoccupations began to replace the holy zest with which Spencer had embarked on his task it scarcely shows. What comes across is an immense sense of involve-ment, of men sharing according to their trades in a vast scheme, each single activity, no matter how menial or homely, contributing to its completion. Spencer conveys the physical details, the spatial relationships of men and

objects, with extraordinary vividness. He gives to his dockyard mateys a speed of movement and dedication not always apparent to the crews of ships they serviced.

By early March 1946, with the completion of *Furnaces*, the series was complete. Spencer had already begun sketches for his Port Glasgow resurrection, the idea for which had developed from his first view of the Port Glasgow cemetery. 'I walked up along the road past the gas works to where I saw a cemetery on a gently rising slope … I knew than that the resurrection would be directed from that hill.' He painted several beautiful landscapes of the Clyde and its surrounding hills while at work on the shipyard. His painting *Port Glasgow Cemetery*, with its uneven rows of white tombstones, its dark clumps of trees, and the Clyde beyond the port in the distance, is not a 'war' picture, but it has a haunting quality similar to certain pictures by Paul Nash and Nevinson painted in Flanders thirty years earlier.

FREETH, T.,
*A Wireless Operator in an Armoured Command Vehicle*, Oil, 18 × 14 ins

# Wyndham Lewis

They have gone into the grey hills quilled with birches
Drag now their cannon up the chill mountains;
But it's going to be long before
Their war's gone for good.

Richard Wilbur, *Mined Country*

Of those others who had fought in the First World War, only Paul Nash made any contribution comparable to Spencer's in the Second World War. Wyndham Lewis was in the United States and Canada, depressed, suffering from eye trouble, short of money, and unable to get home. The War Artists' Advisory Committee contacted him at one stage, when he was surviving by painting portraits of Basilian fathers, but only one picture resulted from it.

Indeed, the correspondence and discussion, not to mention wasted visits to Lewis's studios, required to prise a painting at all out of Lewis were scarcely in proportion to the result.

This fairly farcical episode began with a letter, dated June 10, 1942, to the Committee from Eric Kennington, who reported that Lewis was living in Canada near an aerodrome and would like a commission. On November 23 Lewis wrote from Toronto to the Secretary of Finance: 'I greatly desire to be back in England, but God knows what awaits me there, on the economic plane. The year that preceded the outbreak of war brought me near to bankruptcy in London ... I think of stealing a small motor boat and making a dash for it in the spring. If you hear I have landed in Iceland, you will understand.'

The outcome of this was that Lewis was offered £300 for a commission to be spread over a hundred days. He was, for financial reasons, to be considered a Canadian war artist and he was required to produce one oil or a series of drawings on some aspect of the Canadian war effort. Lewis, though initially demurring at the fee, accepted the offer and set to work. The money was paid.

Over a year went by and no news came from Lewis, who was travelling round Canada keeping going as best he could by painting portraits and teaching. The Committee grew increasingly restless, their requests for information about progress either failing to find Lewis or being ignored. Eventually Malcolm Macdonald, the British High Commissioner in Canada, was induced to contact Lewis. On January 19, 1944 Lewis answered a letter from the High Commissioner, explaining how the conception of his factory subject had changed from 'impressionistic' to 'more solid and detailed and more in harmony with my own tastes and manner of work.' It was going to need much more time. 'It is a busy scene in a factory, with all the contraptions that pertain to such a scene ... what I was looking at was most of the time indistinct as there was a great deal of smoke and steam, and not a great deal of light.'

On November 28 Macdonald wrote to Clark saying that, as far as retrieving the painting concerned, he'd had no luck. 'I am afraid, however, that despite friendly words from my side he now regards me as being in the enemy camp. What a difficult fellow.' Clark had noted on the top of this letter in his miniscule handwriting, 'I fear that we have simply been swindled.'

On June 29, 1945, Lewis—after several letters of masterly prevarication, expressing reluctance for his painting to be shipped during war-time—wrote to the Committee that if 600 dollars could be provided for the passage home of his wife and himself he would bring the picture with him. Clark replied that no more money would be forthcoming.

On August 7 Lewis sailed for Britain on the *Stratheden*, but left the picture behind for separate freighting. On November 28, however, the

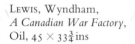

LEWIS, Wyndham,
*A Canadian War Factory*,
Oil, 45 × 33¾ ins

minutes of the War Artists' Advisory Committee recorded that the canvas had finally arrived and that arrangements were in hand for two members to inspect it in Lewis's studio at 29 Notting Hill Gate.

This was the beginning of further delays and stallings, Lewis contriving to be out shopping, ill, away or confused over the dates of appointments. After several fruitless visits to his studio and a series of telegrams from him postponing appointments the picture was taken away—unfinished—on April 1, 1946.

On April 10, Lewis was informed that 'the committee liked your picture so much that Kenneth Clark thinks it should go to the Tate and not to us … I think you may be as well pleased to have it in the Tate as in the Imperial War Museum.'

On April 22 Lewis was writing to Blaikely at the Imperial War Museum about retrieving his picture in order to finish it. 'I shall try and get down on Thursday about noon, and shall hope, while there, to see the sinister treasures of your blood-and-thunder museum. It occurs to me, as I write this, that you could secure fantastic sums in gate money, if only you would advertise on the lines of the fun-fairs. *Horrors of War!* Entrance one shilling (Adults only). One good Salvador Dali could have made the fortune of the museum. But I expect you have nothing more exciting than a house of [*sic*] fire.'

A week later Lewis was writing again to the Committee.

Dear Sirs,

   As you know, my war picture still requires working on. Since this is surely work of a national character and of great importance, I think I should be given some brushes. Hog-brushes I find are unobtainable, but I am told that a chit made out for me by such a body as yourself would secure this essential equipment. Such brushes as I brought with me from America are all worn down to mere stumps.

A series of friendly letters about the loaning of Blaikely's own pre-war hog-brushes was exchanged between Lewis and the Secretary, and the project of Lewis's war picture, initiated nearly four years earlier, was finally disposed of.

The picture itself, *A Canadian War Factory*, an oil measuring $45 \times 33\frac{3}{4}$ inches and representing a scene in a Canadian brass foundry, has only marginal relevance to the war. Most factories were on a war basis. Lewis's painting shows a recognisably helmeted Lewis figure in the left foreground occupied on a task involving chains and pulleys. Vaguely discernible in the background other figures, some possibly women, can be observed busying themselves with a variety of related activities. Lewis has compressed a great deal of machinery and movement into his picture yet the high ceilings and the vertical, furnace-like columns combine to produce feelings of both space and systematised order.

If this solitary work, achieved and deposited eventually in the Tate, seems a modest contribution to Second World War art, Lewis's thoughts on the subject of war and art, his own drawings and paintings of the First World War, as well as a handful of later drawings and oils— *Two Japanese Officers* (a drawing of 1931), *The Surrender of Barcelona* and *The Armada*, oils of 1936 and 1937 in which Lewis, though ostensibly re-creating historical events, suggests inhuman atmospheres and tensions unchanged in modern warfare, and such drawings of the early 1940s as *War News*, a woman looking up with immense sadness from the headlines of a newspaper spread over her lap, and the savage *The Battlefield* and *The Empty Tunic*— all these make Lewis a figure of almost unique relevance in any study of war art.

By the time Lewis, half American, half Scottish-Irish, had joined up as a gunner in 1916, he was known equally as the editor of *Blast*, whose first number had been published in June, 1914, as the author of *Tarr*, and as a painter— founder-member of the Camden Town Group, Vorticist and Cubist.

Late in 1916 Lewis was commissioned and sent to France, where he was in action with a battery near Bailleul. In December 1917 he was appointed a war artist as part of the enlightened Canadian War Memorials scheme. It was in response to this secondment that he produced in 1918–19 the fine oils *A Canadian Gun Pit*, *To Wipe Out* and *A Battery Shelled*, the last however, was for the IWM. Discussing their technique, Lewis remarked in *Rude Assignment* 'War, and especially those miles of hideous desert known as "the Line" in Flanders and France, presented me with a subject-matter so consonant with the austerity of that "abstract" vision I had developed, that it was an easy transition.'

Lewis's main achievement in his war pictures was to give superbly organised abstract compositions a human connotation. *A Battery Shelled* combines the realistic portrayals of a group of foreground soldiers with a number of robot-like background figures. Surprisingly, it works, without loss of either individuality or tension.

In his drawings Lewis set himself the task of portraying 'the gunner's life from his arrival in the Depot to his life in the line.' Thus, in brisk, almost notatory form, he dealt with such subjects as Walking Wounded, The Rum Ration, Siege Battery Pulling In, Shell-Humping, Drag-Ropes, and Morning of Attack. Although recognisably Cubist in manner these drawings have extraordinary mobility and conviction. They are *designed* with all of Lewis's mastery but they convey, quite as powerfully as more realistically produced works, the situation of men under fire. The men, up to a point, are treated as cyphers, but their duties and exposure are real. The devastated backgrounds, with shells exploding violently in no-man's land, serve merely to reinforce and isolate the foreground troops conferring in dugouts or loading their guns. An unmistakably Cubist drawing like *The Attack* achieves the same regular tautness and sense of precipitous movement as Nevinson's best war pictures.

These drawings were shown under the title *Guns* at the Goupil Gallery in 1919. Wyndham Lewis's foreword to the catalogue, in which he discusses war and art, takes up many still relevant themes:

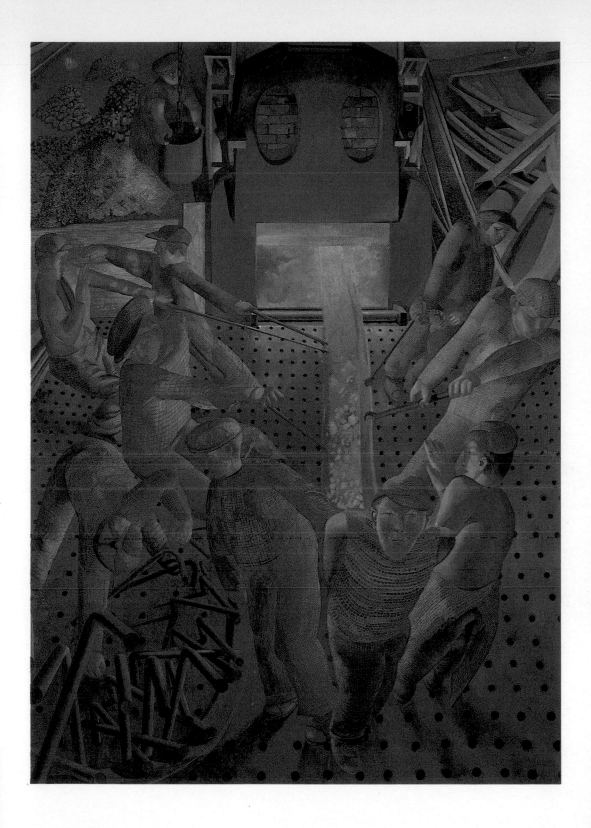

R.A. Commander, Officers, and a District Gunner. Coast Batteries.

Drawn on the coast during September 1940

Whatever we may think about ... it is certain that the philosophy of the War, all the serious interpretation of it, has yet to be done. That could not, for a hundred reasons, be accomplished during the war ... all the War journalism, in painting and writing, will cease with the punctuality and *netteté* of a pistol shot when the war-curtain goes down. It will then be the turn of those with experience of the subject, the inclination, the mood, to make the true record. Truth has no place in action.

This show, then, pretends nothing, in extent ... Experimentation is waived: I have tried to do with the pencil and brush what story-tellers like Tchekov or Stendhal did in their books.

It may be useful to consider war as subject matter, its possibilities and appeals to the artist. Since war-art has been discussed as a result of the universal conditions of war prevailing and since artists, such as were not in the Army, have turned their subject-matter from the Academy rosebud into the Khaki brave ... what artist's name has been most frequently heard?

*Uccello*: that is the name we have most frequently heard ... Detaille, Meissonier were banal illustrators; Verestchagin was a 'war artist' primarily; Uccello was the only great master, in a handy place, who could give us an example of war as subject-matter.

LEWIS, Wyndham, *Walking Wounded*, 1918, Ink, watercolour, gouache, 10 × 14 ins

*opposite above,* ARDIZZONE, Edward, *Naval Control Post on the beaches, Normandy,* 1944, Watercolour, $11\frac{1}{2} \times 18\frac{1}{8}$ ins

*opposite below,* FREEDMAN, Barnett, *The Landing in Normandy,* 1944, Oil, 61 × 120 ins

*overleaf,* GROSS, Anthony, *Battle of Arakan,* 1943, Pen and wash, $14\frac{7}{8} \times 21$ ins

Uccello's battle-piece is a magnificent still-life, a pageant of armours, cloths, etc., the trappings and wardrobe of War, but in the lines and spirit of it, as peaceable and bland as any tapestry representing a civil banquet could be. It does not borrow from the *fact* of War any emotion, any disturbing or dislocating violence, terror or compassion — any of the psychology that is proper to the events of war.

A Japanese warrior, with his ferocious mask, is more frigid than the classic masks of Mantegna's despairing women. Uccello's battle-piece is a perfectly placid pageantry ...

Goya's 'Désastres de la Guerra', a series of etchings done in his old age, is an alternatively sneering, blazing, always furious satire directed against Fate, against the French, against every folly that culminate in this jagged horror. This war-art is as passionate as Uccello's is cold. Both are equally great as painting.

You know Van Gogh's scene in a prison yard? Then you know how he would treat war. You know Velazquez's *Surrender of Breda*? That is his war.

It is clear, then, that an artist of a certain type would ... proceed to arrange Nissen huts, shell-bursts, elephants, commanding officers, aeroplanes, in patterns just as he would proceed with flowers in a vase, or more delectable and peaceful objects ...

Wyndham Lewis was already sixty when he began work on his solitary Second World War commission. The 'jagged horror' he had delineated with such affecting precision twenty-five years earlier had no real counterpart in the art of the Second World War. With few exceptions the artist was no longer in the front line.

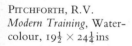

PITCHFORTH, R.V.
*Modern Training*, Watercolour, 19½ × 24¼ ins

# David Bomberg

You would think the fury of aerial bombardment
Would rouse God to relent; the infinite spaces
Are still silent. He looks on shock-pried faces.
History, even, does not know what is meant.

Richard Eberhart, *The Fury of Aerial Bombardment*

William Roberts and David Bomberg, neither of whom found quite the right idiom in their 1914–18 war paintings, were no more fortunate in their efforts a second time round. Bomberg had been transferred in 1917 from the Royal Engineers, with whom he had been serving in France, to the Canadians, with a commission to do a War Memorial painting. His initial treatment of his subject *Sappers at Work under Hill 60* was Cubist, and it was rejected. His second, successful attempt, a powerfully naturalistic version of his Cubist scheme, was much the kind of organised, compressed work, accurately descriptive of men involved in functional tasks, that one would have thought ideally fitted Bomberg to be a war artist in 1939.

He was not slow to apply to the War Artists' Advisory Committee. Two years earlier he had written to Sir Kenneth Clark at the National Gallery recommending that England adopt a similar scheme to the American Works Progress Administration, but Clark had replied discouragingly.

Bomberg's first approaches to the Committee were recorded but no action was taken. He continued to apply for teaching jobs and to the Committee, but nothing came of these applications until 1942, when he was offered a commission to make two drawings of an underground bomb store, for the sum of 40 guineas.

The challenge of painting underground excited Bomberg and he was anxious to start work on a large canvas. For no very obvious reason, the Committee was unenthusiastic, in the way that committees often are, and Bomberg's idea was not taken up. His drawings were purchased but no further commissions materialised.

It is impossible to justify this seeming neglect of Bomberg's talents and enthusiasm. The Bomb Store studies shown in 1981 at the D'Offay Gallery suggest that Bomberg could have produced paintings of relevance and stature with the right kind of direction. His many oil-on-paper sketches, if not derivative of their theme in the most accessible manner, have none the less an edgy, menacing quality, a strident gauntness in their oranges and deep blues suggestive of suppressed violence. The symmetrical paraphrasing of stooped men moving jerkily with lethal loads among bomb stacks is carried out in brilliant colours, redolent of fire and explosion. They convey restlessness, rage and frustration, as if the passion in them could find no release.

In this sense they were probably fair summaries of Bomberg's feelings.

Richard Cork, in a review of the D'Offay show in the *New Standard*, suggested that Bomberg's Bomb Store drawings were studies for an aborted masterpiece, 'it would probably have been the greatest painting to come out of the Second World War'.

Whether, with encouragement, that might have happened, would have depended both on Bomberg's adaptability, and on the provision of a more affecting subject. The Bomb Store drawings do not seem to me in themselves more than indicative of compressed energy, and of how Bomberg's need to be of service could have been utilised. In relation to Bomberg's work as a whole they are of immense interest, but they are portents rather than products. It has been remarked often, by John Rothenstein among others, that many of the best war paintings are of peaceful subjects, of lulls between battles. Bomberg's history put him in a unique position to convey

BOMBERG, David, *An Underground Bomb Store*, 1942, Charcoal, 21 × 26 ins

the particular horrors of the Second World War and unaccountably the chance was let slip. Instead, the last three years of the war were spent dismally, applying, usually unsuccessfully, for teaching jobs, doing ordnance survey work in Southampton and teaching gun crews in Hyde Park to draw. The only compensations were the handful of lushly painted flower pictures done in 1943 and the charcoal drawings of London at night, conceived during the long hours of firewatching.

NASH, John,
*Refitting*, Watercolour,
$14\frac{1}{4} \times 21\frac{3}{4}$ ins

NASH, John,
*Convoy*, Oil, $49 \times 32\frac{1}{2}$ ins

# John Nash, William Roberts, Henry Lamb

Ah, life has been abandoned by the boats—
Only the trodden island and the dead
Remain, and the once inestimable caskets.

Roy Fuller, *The Middle of a War*

John Nash, the younger brother of Paul Nash, had painted *In Oppy Wood, 1917*, and *Over the Top: the 1st Artists' Rifles at Marcoing*, two of the most successful realist pictures of the First World War. He would obviously have been ideal for a second commission as a war artist. But although he was 46 when war broke out he preferred to be more directly involved. After only a few months doing paintings for the Admiralty Nash joined the Marines, serving on the staffs of the Commanders-in-Chief, Rosyth and Portsmouth. In the short periods before and after his service in the Marines, he painted pictures of ships and convoys with the same detached accuracy and calm that for the rest of his life he brought to the delineation of landscape. There is little tension or conflict in John Nash's art, which is as genuinely reflective of a countryman's expert eye as the Ruralist pictures of the 1980s, with their retreat into an artificial Arcadia, seem spurious.

NASH, John,
*Flying Boats*, Watercolour,
$17 \times 21\frac{7}{8}$ ins

ROBERTS, William,
*Soldiers at Train*,
Watercolour, 15 × 21 ins

There remain of the Great War veterans William Roberts, Henry Lamb and Paul Nash. Roberts's *The Gas Chamber*, showing a group of men standing awkwardly about in gas masks—one of a series of smallish watercolours done in 1918—was probably the most successful of his war pictures. Roberts had served for two years in the Royal Field Artillery in France before being made a war artist in 1918. But by 1939—though his methods had scarcely changed since (influenced by the theories of Hulme and Wyndham Lewis) he adopted his idiosyncratic technique of rendering human beings as tubular puppets—he was 44 and less amenable to direction. His mechanistic technique could, in theory, have lent itself effectively to war subjects, but in the end a few portraits, two paintings of women railway porters and station scenes, a Control Room oil and a munition factory poster were all that materialised.

There were reasons for this disappointing haul, the main one, unfortunately, due to a bad misjudgement by Roberts himself. He had offered his services at the outbreak of war promptly and modestly, writing, in a letter of September 12, 1939, of his wish 'to get some pictorial propaganda work to do...am over military age: some two years active service in France during the last war; and was an official War Artist.'

Roberts had been a contemporary at the Slade of Bomberg, Nevinson, Gertler, Wadsworth and Paul Nash among others. His Great War paintings, of which there were half a dozen or so, bearing titles such as *Gas Attack at Ypres*, *Howitzer*, *German Dug-Out* and *A Shell Dump*, suffered from an uneasy adaptation of Vorticist methods. Never as formally striking as

Nevinson's early and best pictures, they lacked the compassion of Paul Nash's. But Roberts had created in the period since the war a sufficiently individual style and subject matter for him to occupy an identifiable position in the art world of the 1930s. His interest in painting not only portraits, but also pictures of people engaged in physical activity — cycling, at the races, playing football, chess, water polo — made him seem ideally suited to the larger themes of portraying troops in action or at recreation. Roberts's art makes its effect by the skilful organisation of groups; the people in his pictures seem to have been painted less for their own sakes than as units in a formal composition. 'His compositions', John Rothenstein has written, 'derive often from those of the tougher Florentines, and in spirit as well as form he has put more than one critic in mind of Pollaiuolo.'

Roberts's request for work was favourably received and before the end of the year he had been commissioned to do six drawings at 10gns each on 'munitions factory' subjects. It was as well for him, for, though the fees were small, he had need of anything he could get. He was teaching part-time at the Oxford Technical School and living at Oxford almost on the breadline.

While discussions were going on about where Roberts was to find his 'munitions factory subject' — Woolwich Arsenal was finally decided on — it was arranged for him to go to France to make drawings of Corps Commanders. Permits and travel passes were fixed up, £20 was paid in advance, a date for the crossing was agreed.

However, on February 8, 1940, Coote at the War Office was astonished to receive the following letter from Roberts:

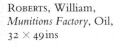

ROBERTS, William,
*Munitions Factory*, Oil,
32 × 49 ins

Dear Mr. Coote,

I have decided to call off my visit to France. Expecting to leave on the morning of the 5th I lost that day as the train did not go until the evening. Arriving at Folkestone I spent a sleepless night in the dining room of the boat ... because no crossings are made at night. Therefore, at seven on Tuesday morning, feeling like anything but a distinguished visitor, I was still in England. As at this hour there was heavy fog (no sailings are made in fog) and no one knew when we were likely to start, I stepped down the gangway, taking the next train to London.

Seeing that I have to do only these drawings and the fee involved is small, it would be better I think if I chose my sitters in England, the people in France could be better dealt with by salaried artists, who will have more time and money at their disposal.

Such a letter was scarcely likely to endear Roberts to his Service employers, but preoccupied with his own parlous financial state, he seems not to have realised it. Coote wrote to Dickey, enclosing a copy of Roberts's letter.

The enclosed copy of a letter from Roberts is rather a shock. It seems to me quite incredible that he should have thought arrangements could be made to suit his personal convenience, irrespective of other considerations. I do not feel inclined, so far as the War Office is concerned, to offer him any alternative employment.

It took Roberts some time to recognise that, far from his own indignation at having to hang around for 24 hours at Folkestone being justified, he had acted foolishly. He was summoned to London and informed that his commission to do drawings of Service personalities was cancelled. The Army wanted nothing more to do with him.

Roberts had already done one portrait, of Major General McNaughton. On March 8 he called at the Ministry of Information complaining he was being badly treated by only being asked to draw workmen. He wanted more 'distinguished' sitters. He did, however, produce two portraits of Woolwich Arsenal workers and was paid for them. A month later he was commissioned to do a portrait of the Minister of Labour, Mr Ernest Brown.

By the end of 1940 Roberts was sufficiently in distress again to have to write to Clark personally, 'Today with the loss of my position as a teacher due to the war I need more than ever this work [the two cancelled drawings]. Cannot the committee be induced to look leniently upon this first offence?'

The Committee suggested to Roberts that he undertake a Civil Defence subject rather than further portraits. The subject of an A.R.P. Control Room in action was put forward, but Roberts replied saying he could not afford to travel unless he received his expenses in advance. 'He is an infernal nuisance', Clark minuted on his letter 'but he is genuinely hard up.'

Roberts was anxious for more work after this application, having believed he had rehabilitated himself. Dickey, however, wrote to him

ROBERTS, William,
*The Control Room, Civil
Defence Headquarters*, Oil,
24 × 28 ins

saying 'funds are not very great' and nothing developed.

In due course, further scraps did come his way. A commission for three drawings of 'war subjects', one of which, a scene at a railway station, was soon delivered. Other projects — tanks being loaded for Russia, allotments, a concert party — failed for one reason or another to come to fruition.

On January 11, 1945, Roberts, after a long silence during which he seems to have ignored letters from the Committee, wrote to them, somewhat optimistically, 'I would like, unless the contract has died of old age, to carry out the drawings I agreed to do some time ago.'

He received, by return, a reply from the Secretary, 'I am afraid your surmise is correct, your contract has unfortunately died of old age. I think you will realize that this was inevitable as it is nearly three years old and my Finance Division cancelled it a long time ago as they took it for granted that you would not be carrying out the work.'

Henry Lamb, 56 when war broke out, was an altogether different case. Charles Harrison in his *English Art and Modernism 1900–1939* describes Lamb's large oil *Irish Troops in the Judaean Hills surprised by a Turkish Bombardment*, 1919, as 'among the most successful of the Post-Impressionist paintings in the Imperial War Museum.' In 1940 Lamb was taken on by the War Office and for the next six years was continuously employed by them on the painting of portraits. These ranged from humble gunners to Generals and Air Marshals. Sympathetic and accomplished though these portraits were, work on them prevented Lamb from all but the most occasional foray into less formal situations. Lamb had served as a Medical Officer in Macedonia, Palestine and France from 1916–1918, winning the M.C.

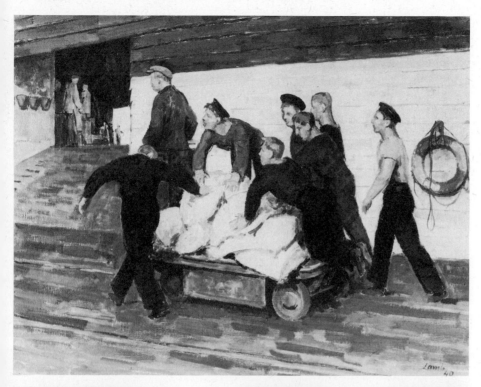

LAMB, Henry,
*The Meat Trolley*, 1940,
Oil, 20 × 25 ins

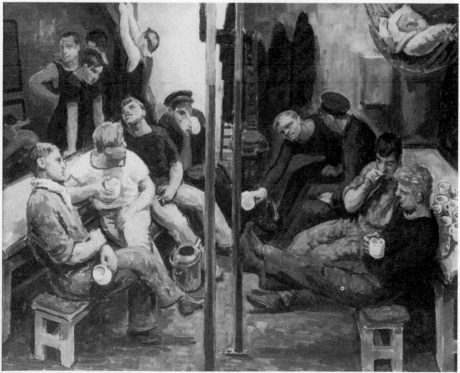

LAMB, Henry,
*Eleven o'clock in Forecastle*,
Oil, 20 × 24 ins

# IV
# THE AERIAL WAR

*Paul Nash*

As a fighter pilot I hoped for a concentration of amusement, fear, and exaltation which it would be impossible to experience in any other form of existence.

Richard Hillary, *The Last Enemy*

From my mother's sleep I fell into the State,
And I hunched in its belly till my wet fur froze.
Six miles from earth, loosed from its dream of life,
I woke to black flak and the nightmare fighters.
When I died they washed me out of the turret with a hose.

Randall Jarrell, *The Death of the Ball Turret Gunner*

Of all English painters in this century Paul Nash is the one who has produced the most memorable images of war. He has, too, described the context, source and intention of his paintings in detailed and evocative language. This is equally true of the work he did in both wars.

Although Nash's involvement in the actual fighting on the Western Front was comparatively brief—he arrived in France as a Second Lieutenant on February 22, 1917 and was invalided home after a fall three months later—the effect on him of the destroyed landscape of Flanders was crucial. In October 1917 Nash returned to France as a war artist, spending a month on the Ypres Salient in the wake of the Battle of Passchendaele. These two visits produced enough work for two shows, one at the Leicester Galleries in May 1918, entitled *Void of War* and containing several oils, the other of drawings under the title *The Ypres Salient*, at the Goupil Gallery in July 1918.

In his posthumously published autobiography *Outline* Nash wrote memorably from Passchendaele of the change in him effected by the butchery of that battle. His first reaction, as a serving officer in a period of lull between battles, had been one of 'excitement and exultation'. *Outline* contains letters, mainly to his wife, full of the familiar exhilaration that derives from an artist having found a subject he can sense is going to work

for him. There was no guarantee that the war would have that effect on Nash, but the brutalisation of the countryside he suddenly found himself forced to contemplate, changed him from a minor landscape painter to one whose images of war had the same tragic intensity, horror and sense of futility as the poetry of the time.

NASH, Paul,
*We are Making a New World*, Oil, 28 × 36 ins

After the initial excitement at so visually strange and suggestive a landscape had worn off, an excitement he transformed into the romantically conceived but honestly felt series of Ypres drawings, Nash felt disgust and despair over what had been done.

The rain drives on, the stinking mud becomes more evilly yellow, the shell-holes fill up with green-white water, the roads and tracks are covered in inches of slime, the black dying trees ooze and sweat and the shells never cease. They alone plunge overhead, tearing away the rotting tree stumps, breaking the plank roads, striking down horses and mules, annihilating, maiming, maddening, they plunge into the grave which is this land; one huge grave, and cast up on it the poor dead. It is unspeakable, godless, hopeless. I am no longer an artist interested and curious, I am a messenger who will bring back word from the men who are fighting to those who want the war to go on for ever. Feeble, inarticulate, will be my message, but it will have a bitter truth and may it burn their lousy souls.

NASH, Paul,
*Moonlight Voyage:*
*Hampden flying above the*
*Clouds,* Watercolour,
20 × 28⅝ ins

The major paintings, oils and watercolours of his return — *The Menin Road,*
*We are Making a New World, Void, Vimy Ridge* among them — attempted
to express this truth. Technically less striking than the early war pictures of
Nevinson and Wyndham Lewis, they are none the less among the most
unforgettable of any pictures that deal with the war.

'A war artist without a war' was how Nash described himself in the early
1920s, his sensibilities having been attacked and refined to a point where
the more conventional concerns of the artist seemed for a time comparatively tame.

In due course, by way of austere Dorset seascapes, abstracts, surrealism
and a very individual concern for objects in relation to landscape, Nash
began to evolve a way of painting that, if it never approached in intensity
his vision of war, nor related as freshly to landscape as his earlier work,
nevertheless often created a strange poetry of juxtaposition. Partly Surrealist, partly derived from his reading and observation of found objects,
Nash's paintings immediately before the outbreak of war have a certain
dreamy coldness and air of contrived expectancy, as if in the inanimate
forms of stones and dead trees he was both remembering and awaiting a
theme. In 1939 Nash painted a largish oil, *Monster Field,* showing a dead
elm trunk in the foreground of a hill-bounded Gloucestershire plain.
Within two years, at a Cowley dump of wrecked German aircraft, he was

able to find a subject with similar formal possibilities but even greater resonance.

In August 1939 the Nashes moved to Oxford and in October Paul Nash founded the Arts Bureau for War Service. It was not long, however, before the War Artists' Advisory Committee approached him, offering him a six-month commission and putting him under the wing of the Air Ministry. A Committee memorandum reports that 'Mr Paul Nash called on June 15 [1940]…he is most anxious to make imaginative reconstructions of aerial fighting and to this end has provided himself with numerous photographs.'

Nash had frequently worked from photographs and his first commission for the Air Ministry was a series of watercolours based on studies of German aircraft that had crashed in woods or cornfields. By September 1940 he had also completed a set of 'aerial creatures', watercolours of British bombers—Blenheims, Hampdens, Wellingtons, Whitleys.

Although these watercolours were warmly received Nash's secondment to the Air Ministry was not happy. Air Commodore Peake, the R.A.F. member on the Committee, was not sympathetic either to him or to his work, and endless bickering developed over fees, materials and subjects.

NASH, Paul, *Bomber in the Wood*, Watercolour, $15\frac{1}{4} \times 22\frac{3}{8}$ ins

This was unfortunate, because Nash had developed a genuine feeling for aeroplanes and the whole business of aerial warfare. On September 17 he wrote to Dickey:

> We are becoming increasingly anxious for London. I hope, desperately, that there is more left of the city and its inhabitants than seems likely from the latest news. For my own part I feel to press on with the job in hand is all I can do so have now evolved a further plan of work which nothing short of an inundation of Nazi termites shall defeat. I may as well confess that my dearest wish is to contribute something useful to the R.A.F by one means or another ... What I do best I believe is what *I* see and am excited about, not what other people see perhaps ... It is therefore very encouraging to hear the Aerial creatures 1st Series 'got over' because that is not an aspect of the airplane which is usually seen.

In the same letter Nash outlines plans for a series of Fighters ('Aerial creatures no. 2'), for a set of drawings dealing with night raids on Germany, and a further series covering the activities of Coastal Command.

It became increasingly apparent, however, that there was a fatal lack of confidence in each other between Peake and Nash. Complaining that his appointment and salary were part-time but 'bloody well whole time' in the demand for work, Nash wrote to Dickey, 'I find Peake unhelpful and apparently indifferent to what I am trying to carry out ... But it is very different when young Squadron Leaders and Station Commanders come to see the work here in the studio. They see the potential value of it and say so with considerable enthusiasm.'

Nash's rather too long and too frequent letters set others beside Peake against him and his commission was not renewed in December. He was understandably upset. 'This is a blow I was quite unprepared for ... I don't want to give up the Air job and its [sic] bloody unfair asking me in the middle of my career.'

In several hurt and exasperated letters to Sir Kenneth Clark he again took up the questions of fees and copyright, comparing his present situation with his pre-war earnings, and stressing his need for expensive drugs. Since the early 1930s Nash had suffered from a form of cardiac asthma that was to kill him at the age of 57. Yet, tiresome though some of his demands undoubtedly seem — especially over the provision of photographs, magazines, newspaper cuttings etc. — there shines through all his writing a real concern over what could be achieved by art in one form or another, and a need to be fully utilised. He was one of the few artists who gave as much thought to the deeper aspects of his relationship to the war as to the painting of his own pictures. 'I want to use what art I have', he wrote to Clark, 'and what I can make as directly as possible in the character of a weapon. I have always believed in the power of pictorial art as a means of propaganda ... Photography is useful, of course, but it is too general, too much taken for granted. Also it is not very intelligently used on our side.'

Clark did his best to deflect Nash's unease and to persuade him that he might, in fact, be better off in future working directly under the Ministry of Information.

I am very sorry you should have had the bother of writing all those long letters to me ... We have told them [the Air Ministry] how foolish they are in very strong — I might almost say insulting — terms, but I am afraid there are a certain number of them led by Peake who yearn for the Royal Academy style, and they are determined to have it. This should not make any difference to you, in fact it may improve your position. You should be able to go on painting flying subjects as much as you like, but for us rather than for your former ungrateful employers.

NASH, Paul,
*Encounter in the Afternoon,*
Watercolour, 15 × 22½ ins

By early January, that is within a few days of the expiry of his Air Ministry appointment, the transfer was effected.

Unfortunately, this did not mean the end of Nash's quibblings over money, privileges and materials. It had to be pointed out to him, fairly forcibly, that he was asking double what any other artist was getting for a picture and that he was being provided with canvases and maintenance. He had no dealer commission to pay on any works bought direct by the Committee and there was, moreover, the question of national service. On February 11 Sir Kenneth Clark wrote to W.G. Crossley of the Ministry of Information, 'I see no reason why we should pay for Mr. Nash's long-distance telephone calls. He has a great liking for such calls and has several times rung me up from Oxford, but never on a matter of urgency. There might be an occasion when a long-distance call was necessary — i.e. if Mr. Nash were arrested for sketching ...'

Nash seems this time to have accepted his mild rebukes with a good grace. It is a relief, nevertheless, to turn from petty haggling in the correspondence to Nash's own description, in a letter of March 11, 1941, to Sir Kenneth Clark, of the painting of *Totes meer*.

> Totes meer. Dead sea. (very much *not* The Dead Sea, of course). Based on actual scene. One of the larger dumps devoted to wrecked German planes alone. You will remember the set of photographs I showed you. The thing looked to me, suddenly, like a great inundating sea. You might feel—under certain influences—a moonlight [*sic*] night for instance, this is a vast tide moving across the fields, the breakers rearing up and crashing on the plain. And then, no; nothing moves, it is not water or even ice, it is something static and dead. It is metal piled up, wreckage. It is hundreds and hundreds of flying creatures which invaded these shores (how many Nazi planes have been shot down or otherwise wrecked in this country since they first invaded?) well, here they are, or some of them. By moonlight, this waning moon, one could swear they began to move and twist and turn as they did in the air. A sort of rigor mortis? No, they are quite dead and still. The only moving creature is the white owl flying low over the bodies of the other predatory creatures, raking the shadows for rats and voles. She isn't there, of course, as a symbol quite so much as the form and colour essential just *there* to link up with the cloud fringe overhead.

In another letter to the Committee Nash observed, 'I should like its title to be given in German and English, Totes meer (Dead sea) note small m for meer and s for sea, 'lifeless sea', really, nothing grand or Biblical about it.

Nash could not have been disappointed by the picture's reception. 'The Dead Sea of wrecked aeroplanes is most beautiful,' Sir Kenneth Clark wrote to him on March 15, 'the best war picture so far, I think.'

It would be hard to quarrel with this verdict, for in *Totes meer* Nash has painted a picture harnessing all the elements under a controlling moon. It is a picture suggestive of irrevocable defeat, of assault and animation halted, brought to a full stop. It is, as Nash was aware and wanted it to be used as such, a very good propaganda picture. But it is much more than that. Its iciness and jagged swirl, its reducing of once beautiful and lethal machines to mere garbage, garbage that might form the waves and undertow of a real sea, create an authentic feeling of chill. Andrew Causey in an essay on Nash in the catalogue to the 1975 Tate Gallery exhibition relates the structure of the picture to Nash's Dymchurch sea paintings of the mid-1920s, as well as to Caspar David Friedrich's *Arctic Shipwreck* of 1824, a picture much revered by the Surrealists. *Totes meer* lives up to its maker's description of it: what Nash felt, and put into words, is all there in his painting. It is quite plain, too, that the whole form of the painting is in the Dymchurch pictures. The wrecked German planes have become simply another element, the earlier pictures almost seeming to have been waiting

for them. In *Totes meer* the planes, as if feeling the pull of the moon, seem to be rising up out of the sea, their wings forming crests. There is a similar rhythm to the planes as to the sleepers in Moore's shelter sketches, wings instead of arms round each other above the blanket of the water.

NASH, Paul, *Totes meer*, Oil, 40 × 60ins

Nash now planned a series of small oils, their subject to be encounters or voyages in the sky, particularly nocturnal ones. In the meantime Hugh Francis, Director of the Photographic Division, Ministry of Information, was having a sharp skirmish with Nash over the latter's reluctance to pay for extra sets of photographs of his work: 'I am a little tired of Mr. Paul Nash and his photographs…In any case experience of Mr. Nash shows that if we give him anything he only asks for more.' This was over a bill for £2 15s 6d.

All Nash's concerns were not for himself. He wrote from Oxford that he had met Bernard Meninsky, who had been 'left without a bean after being sacked by the L.C.C. after 20 years.' Meninsky, undeservedly neglected until his show at Blond Fine Art in 1981, had been a war artist in the First World War. Nash went on, '*I* think he's a very good draughtsman and a sound portraitist. If Roberts is employed couldn't you find old Minky a head or two to knock off? How about Air Commodore Peake's?' Some small commissions resulted.

Nash repeatedly returns in his letters to the question of propaganda. In an undated letter, half of which is missing, he writes,

> This is, before all else, a war of the *imagination*. At first it was called, popularly, a war of *nerves*. That is only another word for imagination … Figuratively speaking, [the enemy] turned the whole world into a vast receiving set which he tuned and adjusted to his various programmes.
>
> Where is *our* imagination, have *we* no ideas, nothing up *our* sleeve. What is needed immediately is a counter imaginative thrust which by its suddenness and novelty will strike straight at the mind as no armoured or explosive missile will at the counter armoured body.

Nash tried at various times to interest other departments in his ideas about pictorial propaganda, many of which seem both sensible and constructive. In May 1941 he made a rare appearance in London, the sight of the bomb damage leading him to write for a permit to do some drawing on his own account. 'Contrary to my expectation I discovered John Piper and Sutherland have not said the last word about ruins.'

For his next large work he offered the Committee a choice of subject, the Battle of Britain or the Bombing of Berlin. They opted for the former and Nash set to work in July on a canvas 48″ × 72″, some eight inches taller than *Totes meer* and twelve inches wider.

The picture was delivered in October and shown at the National Gallery the following January. Nash, as he had done with *Totes meer*, described *The Battle of Britain* in his own words:

> The painting is an attempt to give the sense of an aerial battle over a wide area, and thus summarize England's great aerial victory over Germany. The scene includes certain elements constant during the Battle of Britain — the river winding from the town areas across parched country down to the sea, beyond, the shores of the continent, above, the mounting cumulous [*sic*] concentrating at sunset after a hot brilliant day; across the spaces of sky trails of aeroplanes, smoke tracks of dead or damaged machines falling, floating clouds, parachutes, balloons. Against the approaching twilight new formations of the Luftwaffe, threatening …
>
> Facts, here, both of science and nature are used 'imaginatively' and repeated only in so far as they suggest symbols for the picture plan which itself is viewed as from the air. The moment of battle represents the impact of opposing forces, the squadrons of the R.A.F. driving down the Channel, sweeping along the coast and breaking up a formation of the Luftwaffe while it is still over the sea.

*Battle of Britain* is an altogether more literal painting than *Totes meer*. *Totes meer* suggests more than its ostensible subject. Its themes have to do not only with war — the destruction of once beautiful and powerful machines, the end of aspirations — but with all human life. It is both a symbol and a parable. *Battle of Britain* has no such resonance. It is an action picture pure and simple. On this level it is lively and convincing, and as a composition beautifully balanced. Looking at it, one is immediately involved in the situation, anxious about the outcome. Such scenes were common-place during the late summer of 1940 and Nash has given his aerial battle—the fighters' swirling vapour trails, the black plumes of smoke from a plummeting bomber—a fine flourish. Yet in its detail it is detect-ably a Nash painting. The barrage balloons over the river have the exotic fragility of marine plants, and the sky, in the frenzied scrawl of its contestants, suggests encounters that could equally be between swarms of monstrous insects. It is a painting nicely poised between relish and apprehension.

For some time, despite his bronchial condition, Nash had been making attempts to be taken up in an aeroplane. There was always some set-back or change of plan, and in the end he had to rely for information on talks with pilots, photographs and technical magazines.

He now began making plans for a large picture with a Coastal Com-mand subject. 'I am persistently haunted by a Short Sunderland and I think it will play a large part in the composition.' In the meantime he took up, this time fairly light-heartedly, the question of fees: 'I must regretfully point out that while I may be said to live on air, pictorially, I am afraid I cannot depend on that substance for my existence—more especially as half my time is spent in its artificial manufacture for the purpose of breathing.'

The Coastal Command picture was finally called *Defence of Albion* and is probably the least successful of Nash's four major war pictures. It was the only one that had technical problems which resulted in the picture being returned to Nash for alteration.

'The "goings-on", as it were, of *Battle of Britain*', he wrote 'are equiva-lent to a light-weight activity, even a fly-weight, compared with *Defence of Albion* which is decidedly *cruiser weight or heavy*. It's the colour of a damn cold day on a damn cold sea off Portland—pale greens and queer yellows, steel blues, and then *black* ochre and *white*. Very mouvementé, very lively, regular dust-up.'

As usual, he provided a description of the picture, his motive for this being in part to prevent critics (and others) from making false assumptions about what the painting was supposed to represent.

*Defence of Albion* is a synthesis representing the operations of Coastal Command in the same way that *Battle of Britain* stood incidentally as an epitome of Fighter Command activity ... The Sunderland flying boat [is conceived] as a symbol of defensive attack ... as a powerful and beautiful machine and an aerial creature whose personality suggests something more than mechanical character—something essentially animal and, in a sense, human. In this way the Sunderland—the 'flying battleship' of the English, the 'flying porcupine' to the Germans—becomes in the imagi-nation of the artist a beast as important as the lion or the unicorn in relation to Britain; and for this reason certain features are exaggerated, more particularly in the tail-fin.

The action represented, the sinking of a U-boat by bombing, takes place off the coast of Portland where the rocks are like Cyclopean walls and the white Portland stone is quarried to rebuild what the Luftwaffe have tried to destroy of Albion.

Nash was to paint only one more large picture, possibly his best. 1943, however, was a comparatively unproductive period. He was commissioned, for 60 guineas, to paint four watercolours of aeroplanes. He did three substantial oils, *Landscape of the Summer Solstice*, *Landscape of the Vernal Equinox* and *Michaelmas Landscape*, all scenes of or done from Boars Hill, outside Oxford, and free of war reference. There were projects for paintings with titles like *Arrival of Starlings*, and one showing a flying bomb, to be called initially *A Night Attack*, but Nash could not find a satisfactory point of departure.

In the summer of 1944 he was commissioned to do a sequel to *Battle of Britain*. Nash described *Battle of Germany* to different people at various stages, 'the band of blue is not the sea, it is simply part of a shell-shocked sky ... apart from that, it is absolutely necessary "doing its stuff", just there and just that colour and shape.'

In September 1944 Nash was in the Acland Nursing Home, for what he called, in a letter to Clark, 'rest and reconditioning'. He was very excited about what he now referred to as his *Invasion* painting:

> The new picture is a big job ... I have risked much in it. If it comes off it might be the best thing I have done of any kind. I could not advance it over its second stage without perfect conditions. Now, having studied it and painted it in my mind a dozen times, I feel confident ... Its main lighting is a lunar illumination rather like *Totes meer*, but with brilliant passages of deep red, incandescent pink, and blues. So although it is a night scene it is a brilliantly coloured painting on account of all the explosions going on.

Without Nash's testimony it would not immediately be evident that this paraphrase of an Allied air attack was taking place at night. The prevailing colour is a kind of salmon pink, associable if anything with dawn, not moonlight. However, Nash, describing it in a note dated October 1, 1944, as 'wholly an imaginary scene' but one 'whose elements are based on a careful study of (official) factual evidence' situates it in a detailed poetic context:

> The moment of the picture is when the city, lying under the uncertain light of the moon, awaits the blow at her heart. In the background a gigantic column of smoke arises from the recent destruction of an outlying factory which is still fiercely burning. These two objects, pillar and moon, seem to threaten the city no less than the flights of bombers even now towering in the red sky. In contrast to the suspense of the

waiting city under the quiet though baleful moon, the other half of the picture shows the opening of the bombardment ... In the central foreground, the group of floating discs descending may be a part of a flight of paratroops or the crews of aircraft forced to bale out.

NASH, Paul, *Target Area*, Watercolour, $22\frac{1}{2} \times 30\frac{3}{4}$ ins

*Battle of Germany* is not only the most abstract of Nash's Second World War pictures, it is also the most resolved, its individual elements and happenings absorbed into the underlying scheme. Nash in his description divides the picture into two halves, the waiting city and the approaching bombers, but in practice this division is scarcely apparent. In fact, without Nash's notes, it would be perfectly possible to accept the picture as a semi-surrealist lunar landscape, its areas of violent activity no more than the collision of strange growths or storm clouds. Nash had painted several watercolours and oils earlier in the year of 'giant flowers blossoming among the clouds or sailing down the night skies like falling stars' and *Battle of Germany* is, in many ways, a disciplined adaptation of Nash's metaphysical vision to a war theme. It is a strangely fatalistic, almost serene, painting, the encounter about to take place so familiar and inevitable that there is neither room for manoeuvre nor time for apprehension. The city and its surrounding countryside are a long way below and what happens to its inhabitants is no concern of the pilots. They continue on predestined courses, fulfil their missions, and return home — most of them anyway. The ambiguity of the foreground discs 'a flight of paratroops or the crews of aircraft forced to bale out' is all that intrudes on the sense of confident routine that generally informs the painting. For, essentially, this is a bombing seen from the comparative immunity of the air; in contrast to the Blitz paintings, the early war drawings of Moore and Sutherland, where people are on the receiving end, here the machines are handing it out.

There are few people in Nash's pictures of either war. It is the landscape that is being brutalised in both, and what detritus is left behind after battle is one of machinery not flesh. Nevertheless, Nash's 1939–45 war pictures are on a grander scale, less tied to the specific, to the 'eye-witness' point of view, than anyone else's. Nash thought about what use his pictures could be, not only about what subjects might be rewarding to him as a painter. In this he was truly professional and constructive.

He carried on his epistolary skirmishes with officials to the end. 'I suffer from bronchial asthma', he writes on January 23, 1945 to E.C. Gregory, the new Secretary to the War Artists' Advisory Committee, 'not Delusions or Persecution Mania … and I tell you I have had only one (1) print of *Battle of Germany*. Nevertheless, my kindest regards (and no ill feelings) to you.'

Sadly, the last letter written to the Committee in the large bony handwriting a fortnight later was on the usual topic of money. Enclosing an invoice relating to the transport of *Defence of Albion* Nash wrote, 'I hope I am not too late to "collect" on this … As you see it all relates to a monstrous crate in which to house that painting which no one save its author and a few of the very young seem to care for …'

Nash's work as a war artist, despite continuous bad health and minor frictions, has the double merit of being of its time and integral to his own concerns as a painter. The mood of 1939–45 was totally different from the mood of 1914–18 and Nash's painting reflects the change. Artists have debts to discharge just as do soldiers, sailors, airmen; Nash discharged his, sometimes not without a certain *hauteur*. The sense of human waste and futility is less conspicuous in his paintings of the Second World War, not surprisingly since he was no longer a witness to it. In any case, it was a different kind of war, a defence against racialism and oppression. On the whole, Nash painted syntheses and symbols of the crucial aerial conflicts, tactical wall charts raised to the level of icons.

In the late autumn of 1945 Nash painted his final oil, *Eclipse of the Sunflower*, 'the Eclipse explains itself' he wrote to Dudley Tooth, 'The withered flower head is a ghost of the flower in eclipse or just another sun-flower time has destroyed and the tempest has torn up and scattered over the water.' In January 1946, Paul Nash contracted pneumonia. Six months later he was dead.

EURICH, Richard, *Attack on a Convoy*, Oil, 30 × 40 ins

RAVILIOUS, Eric, *Wake*, Watercolour, $17\frac{1}{2} \times 22\frac{1}{2}$ ins

# V
# SILENT PATTERNS

*Eric Ravilious, Richard Eurich*

How quietly they push the flat sea from them,
Shadows against the night, that grow to meet us
And fade back slowly to our zig-zag rhythm —
The silent patterns dim destroyers weave.

> Norman Hampson, *Assault Convoy*

Don't send me a parcel at Christmas time
Of socks and nutty and wine
And don't depend on a long weekend
By the Great Western Railway line.

Farewell, Aggie Weston, the Barracks at Guz,
Hang my tiddley suit on the door
I'm sewn up neat in a canvas sheet
And I shan't be home no more.

> Charles Causley, *Song of the Dying Gunner*

## Eric Ravilious

It was one of Paul Nash's pupils at the Royal College, Eric Ravilious, who, during the two and a half years he was active as a war artist, did most to record the shape and atmosphere of life at sea — submariners at their various duties, Fleet Air Arm aircraft, coastal defences, convoys, sick bays and guardrooms, aircraft carriers. Richard Eurich and, much later in the war, Leonard Rosoman in the Far East, dealt with different aspects of sea warfare, but it was Ravilious's watercolours painted between 1940 and his death off the coast of Iceland in the autumn of 1942, that depicted in a formal manner naval activity in that period. This activity was conducted almost exclusively in northern waters and Ravilious's paintings suggest the thin skies, the freezing aircraft and guns, the cold seas, with extraordinary fidelity. They are, essentially, designer's pictures, in which the visual 'pattern' — the physical effects of bombs falling in water, camouflaged ships against the horizon, the dispositions of a convoy, the profiles of guns and aircraft — engages Ravilious rather than the human situation. In a sense, the apparent detachment is symbolic: it is the ships and aircraft that dominate the scene, the men who service and control them are mostly invisible. What Ravilious conveys, at the same time, is loneliness and fragility, both of men and machines. The sailors going about their business are cardboard figures, without individuality of feature, and this again helps to reinforce the notion of expendable uniformity. Ravilious shows what sea warfare looks like rather than what it feels like. Nevertheless, his predominantly pale grey, white and Arctic blue watercolours have some of the elegant mysteriousness of Wadsworth's dazzle ship camouflage paintings of 1918. Their fastidiousness and cool clarity are perfectly in keeping with their subjects.

Ravilious was 36 when war was declared. He was born in Acton, brought up in Eastbourne, where he went to the local school of art from the ages of sixteen to nineteen, and then achieved a scholarship to the Royal College. Edward Bawden, Barnett Freedman and Henry Moore were among those there at the time. Ravilious's work during the 1930s ranged from wood-engravings — Bawden considered him the greatest engraver since Bewick — to pottery for Wedgwood and watercolours, mostly landscapes rather in the Nash style. Robert Harling wrote of his 'highly developed decorative sense' and 'fine and austere discipline'.

RAVILIOUS, Eric, *Midnight Sun*, Watercolour, $17\frac{1}{2} \times 22\frac{1}{2}$ ins

RAVILIOUS, Eric,
*Submarine Men*,
Watercolour,
$10\frac{1}{8} \times 12\frac{1}{2}$ ins

At the outbreak of war Ravilious was living with his wife, Tirzah, at Castle Hedingham in Essex. He immediately enrolled in the Observer Corps. In January 1940, he was offered a six-month commission to work as a war artist for the Admiralty and subsequently given the rank of Honorary Captain, Royal Marines, curiously preferring this to the alternative of Lieutenant, R.N.V.R. John Nash, an old friend, who later returned to active service after a start as an Admiralty war artist, wrote rather enviously of Ravilious's 'more varied assignments' and 'unflagging interest in all he saw'.

By February 15 Ravilious was installed in the Royal Naval Barracks, Chatham, and writing to Dickey,

> I have started an exploration of the Dockyards here today ... The people at the docks are rather puzzled but extraordinarily kind and helpful, though I can't really say that there is a great deal in the way of war activity. The place is full of foundries and factories, and fairly soon I think it might be as well to go to Sheerness. Naval and Mess etiquette occupies a lot of my spare time. It is very comfortable living of course but a new recruit has to be on the alert the whole time in order not to make devastating mistakes.

Early in April Ravilious was writing from the Royal Hotel, Grimsby, 'I have given the Admiralty my Chatham and Sheerness drawings and have just arrived here with the idea of going to sea for a few days. My excursions so far have been in very bad weather.'

He made several trips, some as far afield as Norway, and when he was asked to provide pictures for a show of war art to be held in July at the

National Gallery was able to offer paintings of *Ark Royal* and *Glorious*, of Grimsby trawlers, lightships and duty boats, destroyers at night, barrage balloons over Sheerness, and Norwegian ports.

Indeed, in a subsequent letter from Castle Hedingham on H.M.S. *Highlander* writing paper, Ravilious showed a certain embarrassment over how well he was represented at the exhibition compared to everyone else.

In July he was writing from Keppels Hotel, The Hard, Portsmouth, 'I've just arrived at this place, which is almost overwhelming in size and variety—I feel like an earwig setting out to draw Buckingham Palace, though actually I want to try Portland and Poole, and some expeditions perhaps to sea. It is a lively coast just now.'

A month later he was installed in H.M.S. *Dolphin* at Gosport.

At the moment I am living here, having been to sea at different times for the last two weeks in a submarine trying to draw interiors. Some of them may be successful, I hope, but conditions are difficult for work. It is awfully hot below when they dive and every compartment small and full of people at work. However, this is a change from destroyers and I enjoy the state of complete calm after the North Sea—there is no roll or movement at all in submarines, which is one condition in their favour, apart from the smell, the heat and noise. The scene is extraordinarily good in a gloomy way. There are small coloured lights about the place and the complexity of a Swiss clock.

Technically, Ravilious's first commission was over on August 10, but Dickey wrote to him that he could have a month's grace to finish some 'pre-invasion' drawings. He took up residence at the Royal Naval Headquarters, Newhaven, from where he wrote, 'Newhaven is as good as ever: very altered in many ways. I miss the packet boats. I'm concentrating on

RAVILIOUS, Eric, *H.M.S. Ark Royal in Action*, 1940, Watercolour, $16\frac{3}{4} \times 22\frac{3}{4}$ ins

RAVILIOUS, Eric,
*Light Vessel and Duty Boat*,
Watercolour,
16½ × 22½ ins

the fort and the cliffs—pre-invasion drawings of coast defences.' Later he described his south coast interlude in customarily cheery fashion, 'It is marvellous on the cliffs in this weather, though the wind blows a bit, and bombs fall every afternoon, and sometimes planes. One doesn't have to run for shelter as at Portsmouth, so there are fewer interruptions.'

In November 1940 Ravilious's commission was renewed for a further six months, but he was able to spend several months at home in Essex before taking it up. He was hard at work on his submarine and other lithographs, a time-consuming business, for the process involved five workings to each plate. His Newhaven coastal defence drawings had meanwhile run into trouble with the Censor. 'I shall have', Ravilious observed ruefully in a letter to the Committee, 'quite a lot by the end of the war in their vaults and archives.'

By July 1941 the lithographs were done and Ravilious was back in uniform. 'The weather is not what it was', he wrote from the Esplanade Hotel, Dover, 'and a high wind blows, but I rather look forward to doing some more work here after so much hot sun in Essex.'

From the Channel coast Ravilious travelled up in the autumn to the Firth of Forth, where he stayed for some weeks with John Nash and his wife at Dunfermline. Ravilious was much taken with this part of the Scottish east coast, as well as the ports to the north where he later moved. The east coast convoys, which made weekly passages from Rosyth to Sheerness and back, hazarding 'E-boat alley' off the Norfolk/Suffolk shore on each journey, formed up in the Forth estuary. Their destroyer escorts were based at Rosyth, just across the water from Dunfermline. Such paintings of Ravilious's as *Convoy Passing an Island* and *Channel Fisher* are immensely evocative to anyone who served there: the screeching gulls, the harbour craft and cargo vessels pushing to safety under the Forth Bridge,

Section of Interior

RAVILIOUS, Eric,
*Submarine Series:
Different Aspects
of Submarines*,
Watercolour,
$10\frac{1}{8} \times 12\frac{1}{2}$ins

the welcoming flashes of lighthouses and signal stations on May Island and by the Methil roads, the green, tweedy banks of Fife under racing clouds.

'I've just returned here', he wrote on November 15 from Dunfermline, 'from various expeditions. May Island is a grand place — but it is pretty cold work in these parts and I wear all the clothes it is possible to put on and all but burst the uniform.'

By the end of the month he was writing from H.M.S. *Ambrose*, Dundee: 'I'm working at an R.N. Air Station — a very great change from Dover, and can really put down without qualifications that I'm enjoying it immensely. These naval pilots are very good people: and the sea and the Tay look their best though the gales blow every other day.'

To this period belong such works as *R.N.A. Sick Bay, Royal Naval Air Station*, and *Walrus on the Slipway*. He wrote, in a letter sent to the Committee shortly before Christmas,

I spend my time drawing seaplanes and now and again they take me up, this morning rather uncomfortably in the tail, but it was worth it. I do very much enjoy these queer flying machines … I hope Paul N. hasn't already painted Walrus's [*sic*] — what I like about them is that they are comic things with a strong personality like a duck, and designed to go slow. You put your head out of the window and it is no more windy than a train.

RAVILIOUS, Eric,
*Royal Navy Air Station*,
Watercolour,
$16\frac{7}{8} \times 22\frac{1}{2}$ ins

About now Ravilious conceived the idea of paying a visit to the R.A.F. wing in Russia, but for various reasons the project never materialised. He began to feel he had done all he could under Admiralty auspices, at least as far as ships were concerned. 'I don't want to do more naval subjects,' he remarked in February 1942. 'One must stop at some point.' He was taken up by the Air Ministry: 'The Group Captain Lord W. de Broke gave me a wonderful lunch at Boodles of game pie and cake, and is full of good suggestions for this next trip ... Lysanders are the immediate prospect, with the Coastal Command/Sunderlands and Catalinas to follow.'

First stop was the Vale of York, where *Aeroplanes on an Airfield* was painted. Ravilious's sense of the vulnerability of grounded machines, their inadequacy and clumsiness when deprived of their proper element, infects nearly all his aircraft paintings. Even flying, as in *H.M.S. Glorious in the Arctic*, they seem toy-like, soaring and gliding as if catapulted by school-boys.

From the Vale of York Ravilious moved south to the R.A.F. station at Sawbridgeworth, in Hertfordshire. Here he drew Spitfires waiting for take-off and pilots doing elementary flying training on obsolete machines. His painting of the latter, showing trainee and instructor in an old dual control machine flying low over a Hertfordshire field — camouflaged hangars, water-tower, clumps of trees, long grasses — is typically Ravilious in its affectionate amusement. The plane seems almost stationary, as if suspended from the sky on wires as in a theatre backdrop. The battle areas may be a long way off, but this, tenuously, is where it all begins. In most of Ravilious's war pictures ships and sea, aircraft and landscape, blend together, camouflage having transformed machinery and nature into a single abstract.

In June 1942, Dickey wrote to Ravilious, 'Two subjects are proposed for you by the A/A Committee when you can spare the time from your air activities. The first is the concealment of white horses and other such images cut in chalk, and the second fire engines spraying with ink chalk railway and road cuttings.'

Ravilious was mildly enthusiastic about these curious notions, but, though he went to Uffington to have a look round, before he could get started Dickey informed him that these experiments were not being repeated and therefore it was 'hardly appropriate to record' them.

Dickey retired from the Secretaryship of the Committee later that summer and Ravilious attended his farewell party, returning late at night with 'Barnett [Freedman], Harry Moore, and Sutherland in high spirits.'

On July 22 Ravilious wrote to Palmer, Dickey's successor, 'I may go off to Iceland if Lord W. de Broke can arrange that … I'd like to visit the Norwegian squadron.'

On August 25 Ravilious left London by air for Iceland. A week later he took off as a passenger on a reconnaissance flight. The plane was never seen again.

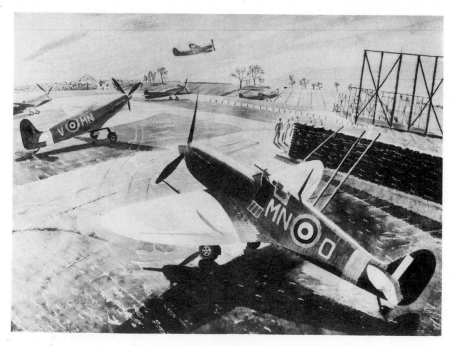

RAVILIOUS, Eric,
*Spitfires — Early Morning*,
Watercolour, $18 \times 24\frac{3}{8}$ ins

Before the war Ravilious was an elegant decorative artist in various media. The war was not an interruption to his work so much as a deepening of it. The designer remained evident in all his war pictures, but his enthusiasm for and curiosity about new experiences gave his decorative skills a fresh context. He came into his own, absorbed and enchanted by the strange relationships between submarines and their crew, aircraft carriers and planes; by light on water, the intricacies of sophisticated equipment, the sight of ships at speed. Ravilious painted 'Home Fleet' weather: the Arctic and North Seas, the Channel. His skies are gusty, the sun remote. His subjects included such items as 'De-Icing Aircraft'.

Ravilious's is not a warm art, nor would it probably have been in tropical conditions. The north suited him. All his paintings are original in conception, unmistakably his in their point of departure, their clean quality of line, their neat cross-hatching, their balance of light and shade. There is no mess in them, none of the rough intrusiveness of humanity, the awkward presence and litter of individuals. They have the courtesy and detachment commonly associated with the service to which he was mostly attached.

It was unfortunate that, during the six months in which Ravilious was only 'presumed dead', his widow had to devote so much energy to getting compensation. She had Ravilious's 85-year-old father to provide for, and their own children to look after. Her income was £11 a week. Ravilious had left one finished picture and three unfinished. There was a small mess bill left unpaid and some salary owing. But reading the endless letters that travelled to and fro between departments over paltry sums is to be made to realise that bureaucracy is not concerned with feelings. Mrs Ravilious, in the end, got what was considered to be proper in the circumstances. The Committee expressed its sympathy and did all it could. But Finance departments proceed strictly according to rules and war artists were not really expected to get killed, especially, as in this case, between commissions. For, as it turned out, approval for Ravilious's fourth commission had not officially come through on the day that he was reported missing. The dates had, in the end, to be 'adjusted', so that provision could be made. The long and drawn-out wrangle was yet another instance of the anomalous circumstances in which war artists often found themselves.

# Richard Eurich

Tonight the moon has risen
Over a quiet harbour,
Through twisted iron and labour,
Lighting the half-drowned ships.
Oh surely the fatal chasm
Is closer, the furious steps
Swifter? The silver drips

From the angle of the wake:
The moon is flooding the faces.
The moment is over; the forces
Controlling lion nature
Look out of the eyes and speak:
*Can you believe in a future*
*Left only to rock and creature?*

Roy Fuller, *Harbour Ferry*

Richard Eurich was exactly the same age as Ravilious. Other than that, and the fact that both were attached to the Admiralty, they had little in common. Ravilious, though brought up on the Sussex coast, became involved with the sea as a subject largely through the accident of war. Eurich had established himself near Southampton Water long before the war and such places as Lyme Regis and Chesil Bank were native to him. As a student at the Slade — where he had been a contemporary of William Coldstream, Claude Rogers and Rex Whistler — Turner had been the painter he had most admired. His first show, at the Redfern in 1932, was mainly of ships and seascapes, influenced partly by Christopher Wood, whose subsequent death was a great blow to him.

Eurich was born in Bradford, of Quaker stock, German in origin. As soon as war broke out he volunteered for service as an ambulance driver. In the spring of 1940 he was approached by the War Artists' Advisory Committee and sent off to paint fishing boats at Whitby. Having fulfilled that commission he suggested that he might be allowed to tackle the subject of Dunkirk, since it was an area he knew well from a visit the previous year. It was typical of Eurich that he should have suggested an epic theme. He had written, 'It seems to me that the traditional sea painting of Van de Velde and Turner should be carried on', and most of his more ambitious war paintings were set pieces on the grand scale — *Great Convoy to North Africa, Preparations for D-Day, Mulberry Harbour* and *Night Raid on Portsmouth Docks*. He had always, he wrote, been interested in the 'structure of water', having spent hours watching and memorising the sea against jetties and the Atlantic rollers at Chesil.

His Dunkirk painting met with approval and was purchased. He described it in these terms, 'Troops are being taken off the beaches in all kinds of craft, in a restless swell under a clear sky. Over the town itself the fires which burned for days have raised a monstrous pillar of black smoke which hangs in the windless air.'

Eurich saw it as his task to record events as accurately as possible, not by symbols or sign language, but by the precise rendering of detail. He consciously adapted his technique, achieving clarity of composition and depth of focus as if adjusting binoculars. He had no need of photographs, relying on a photographic memory and drawings done on the spot, many of them in a personal shorthand more evocative to him than if they had been fully realised.

Portsmouth and Southampton took a battering in 1940–1, and Eurich, living so close, was able to observe the effects of bomb damage at first hand. Often he bicycled over to Portland, a journey he made every day for two months while he was working on his 1940 picture *Air Fight over Portland*.

> The scene is Portland, September, 1940, when over 40 German aircraft were brought down in a very short action. The bombers are coming up through the thin cloud protected by fighters only just visible above them. Our fighters have already dived through them and shot some down...One German bomber has come down in the roads. Two Germans are seen descending by parachute. The white condensation trails in the sky show where the fighters have been at work. The ruins in the foreground are those of a castle built by Henry VIII.

Paul Nash's descriptions of the content of his war pictures lead one into and through ambiguous areas. There is no ambiguity in Eurich's art and so, in a sense, his accounts of what is taking place are gratuitous. Everything

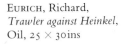

EURICH, Richard,
*Trawler against Heinkel*,
Oil, 25 × 30ins

can be seen, for he has taken great pains that this should be so. Yet if he became, at least for the duration of the war, a completely literal artist, he was never a dull one. His close relationship to the sea, his attempt to understand and paint it scientifically rather than impressionistically, give his paintings an extra credibility. Eurich's paintings in the late 1970s, especially those of figures on beaches, have an almost mystical, hieratic quality and the handling of forms and surfaces makes them instantly recognisable. This was not the case with his war pictures, where individuality of brushwork and approach has been sacrificed for definition. It is as if his pictures were going to be scrutinised for their Intelligence value.

Eurich wrote of the sea, 'I felt it as a symbol of a certain loneliness which I have always desired and the sight of the sea has always brought that constriction of the throat caused by something of indescribable beauty.' It is to Eurich's credit that he put so romantic an attachment to so analytic a test.

No other painter of sea warfare has got so much into his pictures, in which events are seen both anecdotally and as at the end of a telescope or through bridge glasses. The skilful organising and ordering of so much activity, apparent in all his large paintings, gives them a sweep that is truly epic. At a time when any such methods were not only unfashionable but full of hazard it says much for Eurich's powers of application that he was able to bring off at least one such painting a year, in addition to numerous smaller works.

Once the invasion scare was over Eurich took passage in destroyers operating in the Channel. 'You could see the French coast and you could see the Dover coast and you felt you were sort of on the curve of the world.' He was never seasick, whatever the conditions, and he was able to contemplate and convey, as a consequence, rough seas without too evident a distaste. In pictures like *Destroyer Picking up Survivors* and *Survivors from a*

EURICH, Richard, *A Destroyer rescuing Survivors*, 1942, Oil, 30 × 40 ins

*Torpedoed Ship* he suggests with great force the loneliness of men exhausted by the elements, at truly their last gasp. The survivors' situation is the pictorial and dramatic focus of the painting, yet every inch of the ocean—the waywardness of the waves' flow and fall, the curdled valleys beneath crests, the screens of spray—is realised as if it were also crucial. The same is true of the sky.

In most of Eurich's large-scale paintings men are necessarily subordinate to the scene. But in *Destroyer Picking up Survivors* this is only partially true, for the ten or so sailors in the boat are painted in Breughel-like detail, their expressions and the attitudes of their bodies indicative variously of fear, exhaustion, approaching death, intense activity, disbelief, amazement.

1942 saw the completion of four of Eurich's most important paintings: *The Raid on Vaagso*, *The Raid on Bruneval*, *Great Convoy to North Africa* and *Night Raid on Portsmouth Docks*. The Portsmouth painting was done from the Signal Tower, its topography 'pretty accurate though telescoped a bit in places'. Eurich made the drawings for this on a day after particularly heavy bombing, the German bombers attracted by the presence of two battleships in the harbour.

In *Great Convoy to North Africa* Eurich used the 'wide-screen' angle adopted by Ivon Hitchins for his landscapes and by most film makers a decade later. In all these paintings of 1942 Eurich is recording a historic scene, bringing together all its constituent elements in a historic panorama. It is an intention dramatically opposite to that of most war artists whose taste—in which they were encouraged—was for incidental or routine activity visible at firsthand, and in many cases organically related to the

EURICH, Richard,
*The Raid on the Bruneval
Radio-location Station,
27th–28th February 1942*,
Oil, 30 × 40 ins

themes of their pre-war painting.

It is symbolic that the Great Convoy picture, showing the departure in November 1942 of 800 ships packed with troops, should be presented through field-glasses. For this binocular vision is typical of Eurich's war art. It is a vision, moreover, very true to that of most naval personnel who relied on powerful glasses to scan the horizon for U-boat periscopes, mines and unidentified shapes. The frozen clarity obtained from these strong lenses is reflected in the definition of Eurich's painting.

Eurich's last major war painting has as its subject the assembling of a pre-fabricated Mulberry harbour. All through the winter of 1943–4 preparations for D-Day were observable along the south coast. Eurich painted the Mulberry harbour after making a number of drawings on an escorted tour. 'They wouldn't tell me what it was for but they took me out in a duck ... it was like a lot of factories standing up out of the water.'

For Eurich, as for most painters who had been involved from the start, the war began to pall as a subject, especially the need, as he saw it, for 'exactness'. At the end of March 1945, a mere five weeks before V.E.Day, he wrote to the Committee, 'I have hardly started to live this year yet ... I haven't done a painting, drawing or study of any kind for my own edification for a couple of years.' This was in contrast to many war artists (Paul Nash among others) who were able, in between commissions, to paint for themselves.

Eurich's father and younger daughter had recently died within a fortnight of each other. He himself was suffering from sinus trouble. He had certainly earned a rest, after so long, from dock installations and ships.

EURICH, Richard,
*Preparations for D-Day*,
1944, Oil, 30 × 50 ins

Eurich later wrote that he painted his war pictures from a 'different part of me'. In the immediate post-war period he felt, nevertheless, rather a fish out of water. His old gallery, the Redfern, was showing a quite different kind of painting. It was nearly twenty years—and several movements in art later—before Eurich found a real response to what he was doing. He showed several times at Tooths and the Fine Art Society, as well as at the Royal Academy. Curiously, his subjects were again mostly marine—tankers, bathers, beach-scenes. But the 'need for exactness' had gone and in his paintings of the late 1960 and 1970s Eurich was able to give the Hampshire and Dorset coasts, which he has never left, a more human and domestic context.

# VI
# EXERCISE CANDLE
*Albert Richards*

> For here the lover and the killer are mingled
> who had one body and one heart.
> And death who had the soldier singled
> has done the lover mortal hurt.
>
> Keith Douglas, *Vergissmeinnicht*

'All British paratroops trained in England', Albert Richards wrote on September 1, 1943, describing one of his paintings to the Secretary of the War Artists' Advisory Committee, 'know the meaning of "Exercise Candle." It means the change from being a parachutist to becoming a paratroop.' He continued 'Last year and this year, until I joined the paratroops, my mind was very blank and I hadn't any desire to paint. Now that my life is more interesting I haven't the time to paint. But I have the beautiful experience of parachute descents to make up for it.'

That 'beautiful experience' was the main subject of Richards's unique contribution to war art. When he was killed on March 5, 1945, crossing a minefield in his jeep, he had been an official war artist exactly a year. In that time he produced a body of work whose immediacy and vivid depiction of battle landscapes placed him more closely to the war artists of 1914—18 than any other of his contemporaries. Richards followed the Allied armies from the D-Day landings through France and Holland in the closest association. In the paintings of his last year you get not only a front line view of gliders landing, paratroops dropping out of the sky, demolished bridges and burnt-out German petrol tankers — the various species of country fought over by advancing and retreating armies — but you sense the presence of death. This is not a frequent sensation in the work of war artists, for commonsense and practical reasons. But in Richards's pictures the Germans have not long been gone and what they have left behind, in men and *matériel*, has the freshness of war about it.

Before he was appointed a war artist Richards had served four years in the Army, first as a sapper, then as an engineer parachutist. In this, too, Richards's experience resembled that of several First World War artists, Paul Nash among them. It is ironic that it should have been as a war artist, ostensibly freed from the involvement and obligation of a fighting soldier, that he should have met his death.

Perhaps stranger still is Richards's fascination with the figure of the parachutist, a fascination that began in art—pictures by Christopher Wood and Paul Nash—and which ended with his becoming the figure himself. Allen Freer, in his Introduction to the catalogue for 'The Rose of Death', an exhibition of Richards's war paintings shown initially at the Imperial War Museum in 1978, relates a pre-war, rather Craxtonish gouache of Richards's called *Drummer and Monkey Parachutists* to a late painting of Wood's called *Zebra and Parachute*. Parachutists figure in other Richards's engravings and paintings of 1938–9. Freer quotes effectively from one of Paul Nash's essays in *Outline*:

> When the war came, suddenly the sky was upon us all like a hawk hovering, threatening. Everyone was searching the sky expecting some terror to fall; I among them scanned the low clouds or tried to penetrate the depth of the blue. I was hunting the sky for what I most dreaded in my own imagining. It was a white flower. Ever since the Spanish War, 'the rose of death', the name the Spaniards gave to the parachute, had haunted my mind so that when the war overtook us, I strained my eyes to see that dreadful miracle of the sky blossoming with these floating flowers. The first picture I made of the War was a collage of the Rose of Death.

In works by Richards like *The Drop* and *The Landing H hour minus six*, both painted in 1944, Nash's romantic notion of 'floating flowers' gets grimly practical expression. In *Parachute Jump near Tatton Park* (1943), in its way one of the most tensely realised and dramatic pictures of the war, all sense of fantasy and symbolism has dissolved before the falling figures' total concentration on technique, hands tight to the thighs, feet close together, body pulled slightly forward into an open jack-knife position by the opening parachute. The men on training exercises portrayed in *The Drop* and *Parachute Jump near Tatton Park* belonged to battalions dropped in Normandy on D-Day. Richards's own assumption and acting out of the parachutist's role is an extraordinary reversal of the customary relationship between nature and art.

Like Wilfred Owen, Albert Richards came from Merseyside. He was born in Liverpool, the son of a wood-worker who had served in France during the First World War. In 1925, when their son was six, the Richardses moved to Wallasey. Here Albert Richards spent his whole childhood and adolescence, moving from Wallasey School of Art on a scholarship to the Royal College only after the war had started. He had scarcely been at the Royal College three months when he was called up for National Service, but it was long enough for him to take the eye of Paul Nash and for the work of Spencer, Ravilious and Bawden to replace the Surrealist influence of his Wallasey days.

Richards, along with other painters older than himself—William Scott,

RICHARDS, Albert, *The Drop*, Oil, $21\frac{5}{8} \times 29\frac{5}{8}$ ins

Keith Vaughan, Rodrigo Moynihan among them—took time to adapt to Army life. He began his training in Suffolk, moved up to Northumberland for bridge-building exercises, and then, in the spring of 1941, was drafted south, first to Wiltshire and finally back to Suffolk. By this time he had set his heart on becoming a paratrooper. His repeated efforts prevailed and in the spring of 1943—by which time he had been in the Army three years—he was accepted for training in 591 (Antrim) Parachute Squadron based at Ringway, Manchester. Here, in the indoor parachute training school directed by Wing Commander J.C. Kilkenny, pupils went through, in simulated conditions, the motions of jumping from an aircraft.

By the time Richards arrived at Ringway he had completed over twenty pictures based on his experiences as a sapper. Their subjects ranged from anti-tank ditches and camouflaged huts to gun-sites and searchlight batteries. He submitted successive batches of them to the War Artists' Advisory Committee and eight of his oils were bought, though none of his watercolours.

Other artists, besides Richards, began to run out of subjects, either as serving soldiers or when confined to Britain, where, after the aerial battles of 1940–1 and the Blitz, there was evidence of preparations for war rather than the event itself. The new sensation of parachuting changed everything for Richards. As with Peter Lanyon, killed a decade later when gliding, the aerial view, scooping up and smoothing out chunks of land, produced an exhilarating visual experience.

The ground, once seen with all its ugliness and imperfections, was now a remote drifting region of spilled yellows, greens and browns, the sky tilted and the body freed.

Richards's parachute paintings express, more than anything, a feeling of release: release from the body's weight, but also from petty human involvement. They are not carefree paintings, all the same, for this heavenly free-fall is not some aerial game but a skilled technique with specific objectives. There is no vague symbolism any longer attached to the opening rose. Death may well be at the end of it, but in the meantime men have to come to terms with their dependence on and control of a fragile piece of equipment. On its reliability their lives—and the outcome of crucial battles—depend.

Richards's first parachute pictures, done in the spring of 1944, were of training exercises, based on his experiences at Ringway and at various bases in southern England where rehearsals for D-Day were in full swing.

From No. 5 PR Service, 21 Army Group, Richards wrote to Gregory of the Committee:

> I feel that I should write to you, at this hour of the day when the summer evening is preparing to give way to twilight. In a few hours time I start upon my job as 'Official War Artist'. I am certain that should I have the good fortune to come through this operation, I will be in the position to send some good paintings to you. The subject is very good. I have been very fortunate to be in on it, and I feel that I will really be fulfilling the task I set out to do, e.g. to produce paintings of the war and not preparations for it ...
> Tomorrow I shall be in France. The beginning.

Richards parachuted into Normandy with the 9th Battalion, 6th Airborne Division. On a brief return visit to England he wrote to Gregory:

> I have come back to England to collect my kit which I was unable to take with me on the Airborne Invasion. During my stay in France I was able to make a few sketches during the quiet periods, which were all too few, where the paratroops were concerned.
> Whilst waiting to return to France, I have made a few watercolour drawings. I'm not sure of their value. In painting them my mind was always full of pictures of my gallant Airborne friends who gave their lives so readily. It's the first time I have ever witnessed death in this crude form. Somehow I am hoping that it will all help me to paint the pictures I want to paint yet feel so unable to do so. I feel that watercolour transparent and opaque will be the best medium for me to use at this stage of the battle.

This letter was followed by another describing the watercolours he had mentioned:

RICHARDS, Albert,
*A Searchlight Battery*,
Oil, 20 × 30 ins

(1)  The Landing—H hour minus six. In the distance the glow of the Lancasters bombing the battery to be attacked.

(2)  Withdrawing from the battery, after the battery's guns had been destroyed. The M.O. set up his R.A.P. in a bomb crater.

(3)  At the village of Le Plein the constant watch for snipers hidden in the village.

(4)  Gliders cross-landed against bridge.
Occupants took bridge which is one of our two vital bridges which form the link between the main 'bridge-head' and the eastern sector held by the Airborne.

In the immediacy of their evidence, quite apart from their painterly merits, these watercolours are of unique interest. Richards ended his letter: 'At present I'm on my way back to France. I shall spend a couple of weeks finishing off the work with the "Airborne", then I am following up the land-forces.'

He was writing again to Gregory on July 19:

I know the four watercolours I sent in to you were much below what I expected of them. I was in rather a dazed condition when I painted them…The method which the committee suggests I work is the method which I have been brought up to. The Design School at the R.C.A. was a great believer in giving the subject time to develop before putting any statement on paper. I have always felt that if the subject was good enough, it would still be as fresh months after seeing it, and probably would have developed in one's mind during that time.

In the same letter Richards mentions the possibility of getting a lift on one of the cross-channel planes taking the wounded to England. Although this does not seem to have materialised, what he had in mind was talking over his work with Sir Kenneth Clark and calling on the Committee whose Secretary had written sympathetically to Richards, counselling him to take his time and not to rush his experiences into paint before he was ready.

Richards continued to work in watercolours, 'there is much to be said in this medium,' at the same time feeling, without justification, that what he was doing was not very good. The Committee did their best to put his mind at rest.

Subjects in this batch included crashed gliders at Ranville, exhaustion cases in wide, canvas-covered trenches, night scenes at La Délivrande (where the 6th Airborne Division were holding the northern end of the Normandy bridgehead) and the Délivrande public garden turned into a giant car park. 'In a single day 15,000 vehicles passed one check point, the equivalent to one every five seconds.'

On August 14 Richards wrote again to Gregory:

Lt. Hennell, who lives in the same house as myself, has returned here safely from England…We have been used to working up to eleven o'clock. The daylight now lasts to about ten o'clock, but we have been rewarded by the beautiful evenings, when the countryside is bathed in soft hues of pink and blue. The end of August will see the end of my six months…I would, very much, like to continue with my work. Do you think this is possible? The six months has been a great experience to me, from which I feel certain I shall benefit. My first impressions of France are beginning to change. I am forming a liking for the people, and the flat landscape does not annoy me nearly so much as it did at first.

Richards was granted his wish and his commission was extended. The autumn and winter of 1944–5, the last six months of his life, were short of letters but rich in painting. The Allied armies fought their bitter way east, across Belgium and Holland. Richards, mostly in watercolour but with occasional oils such as *German Bridge Demolition*, recorded the litter of retreat and the devastation of advance. There are few human casualties in these pictures; instead Richards has placed dead livestock and lost-looking civilians in contexts that suggest homelessness, the ruin of the countryside, family loss.

It was not until January 19, 1945, that the Committee again heard properly from Richards:

Dear Mr. Gregory,
    I have sent you some of my recent work. I wanted to start the New Year without the old year's finished work upon my hands. There are six paintings in oil, two in watercolour, and one small watercolour, which for some reason I like, so I may send that also. The Siegfried line has

interested me. One painting of it is amongst the six oil paintings. I was, when making notes on this line, living in Sithard, a place I have returned to after a spell in the Ardennes. I stayed with the Sixth Airborne Division and lived for a short while with the Bn. I came to Normandy with. With me was Ian Struthers (Paramount News), nephew of Eric Kennington. We stayed in the village of Bande. This is the village where the Germans murdered 39 of the men of the village. The bodies of the victims were discovered by members of the Airborne Divn. I made notes on the bodies and the scene of the bodies being put into coffins. Also on the funeral, where the feelings of the women folk of the village were expressed in sobs and bitter crying, wailing. I hope to be able to make some paintings on the notes I have made in this village.'

Richards's last, undated letter was sent to Gregory not long before his death:

The cold spell ended very rapidly here, as it did in England. Spring, although a month ahead of us, is very much in the air.

 Advances are happening at different points in the line. So much so, that one is inclined to hop from one sector to another. The landscape is becoming more interesting as we climb out of Holland and into Germany. The flooded landscape has brought fresh interest to the warfare. Warfare that amounts to island hopping on a small scale. The past few

RICHARDS, Albert, *Holland 1944, Infantry of the 15th (Scottish) Division taking over*, Oil, 32 × 30 ins

RICHARDS, Albert,
*Erecting Pickets*, Oil,
20 × 32 ins

*opposite above,*
EURICH, Richard,
*Fortresses over*
*Southampton Water,*
1942, Oil,
14½ × 50 ins

*opposite below,*
RICHARDS, Albert,
*The Industrial Battle,*
Oil, 20 × 30 ins

*overleaf above,*
RICHARDS, Albert,
*Crashed Gliders,* 1944,
Watercolour,
21 × 28¾ ins

*overleaf below,*
CARR, Henry, *Vesuvius*
*in Eruption,* 1944, Oil,
14½ × 21½ ins

days have been very enjoyable, taking small voyages across these flooded areas. Slowly but surely we are creeping into Germany, one might say into Germany in bottom gear which surely applies to driving in a jeep, for if it's not traffic that holds one up, it's the muddy roads. I'm not very good at traffic hold-ups which I suppose are inevitable, and I've developed the bad habit of trying to find a new road. On our map there are several possible routes, and I try them. This is where the badness of the habit shows up. For I usually end up at a blown bridge and have to return to the traffic-jam, or I get my car bogged in some deep mud, miles from help ...

I am concentrating more on watercolour as it is easier to handle in difficult conditions, and making notes on subjects I should like to paint in oils, to [be] painted where suitable conditions prevail. Several people I know tell me they have met Tom Hennell but so far I seem to miss meeting him.

The press seems to be in a very hopeful mood regarding the progress of the war. People talk about seeing the RAF damage to Berlin. To me, the fighting seems to be the hardest we have met in the war.

Perhaps it is the end. Thank you once again for your letters.

Within two months it was, in fact, all over, but the 'bad habit' had this time led Captain Albert Richards and his jeep, on the tail of the retreating Germans on the banks of the Maas, into a minefield, not merely a blown bridge.

More than any other painter of the war Richards had grown up through it from virtually a student into an artist of stature. Almost every other

painter who worked as a war artist had work behind him on non-war themes. For Richards the war was his only real subject.

'Whatever premeditation lay behind his watercolours and final oil paintings', Allen Freer observed, 'is hidden in the wiriness of his line and the vibrancy of his colour. His handling of the paint has a largeness, a generosity of gesture that is at once buoyant and dramatic as if a febrile energy of thought and execution were his for the asking. He had found "the dominant of his range and state" in war with which he identified his vision and his gifts.'

Robin Ironside in *Painting Since 1939* spoke of Richards's 'personal, curious gaiety of colour that spreads over his pictures animating every part so that they produce a kind of vernal glitter in which their subjects, mainly incidents in the land war, are effaced.'

'Generosity of gesture' and 'vernal glitter' are certainly characteristics of Richards's war paintings. Like most of the best writing about the war, whether poetry or prose, Richards's painting is factual and emotionally low-key, concerned more with the shape and feel of mechanised warfare than with ideologies or corpses. The effects of war, in Richards's pictures,

*opposite,*
ROSOMAN, Leonard, *A Damaged Corsair Aircraft on the Flight Deck of H.M.S.* Formidable, Gouache, $15\frac{1}{4} \times 20\frac{1}{2}$ ins

*overleaf above,*
PITCHFORTH, R. V., *Activities begin as soon as mist blows out to Sea,* Watercolour, $21\frac{1}{4} \times 29\frac{3}{4}$ ins

*overleaf below,*
ROSOMAN, Leonard, *A Black Aeroplane on a Red Deck,* Gouache, $15\frac{1}{2} \times 18\frac{3}{4}$ ins

RICHARDS, Albert, *An Anti-tank Ditch,* Oil, $23\frac{1}{2} \times 31\frac{5}{8}$ ins

are everywhere evident, on orchards, on river-banks, on small villages. What he was recording were the last stages of simultaneous defeat and victory in what never seemed to him other than a just war. Richards's art is neither a questioning nor a tortured one. The casualties and the destruction he witnessed were part of an inevitable process it was his task to paint. This involved working at great speed, looking selectively and knowing what he was looking at. In this last respect his professional training as a sapper and a paratrooper was invaluable.

Although Richards's war art is as nearly extravert as such an art can be — the marginalia of a fighting soldier — it is never detached or cold. The colours, for example, tend to be rich and involving, singing yellow, warm orange, lime greens. The canvas is tightly organised, packed with action. The feeling is of simply a pause in a vast co-ordinated effort of which the painter has chosen to compress and freeze an instant.

But what specifically lifts Richards's images of the Allied landings above even the best kinds of documentation is the sense of his own involvement. His are images that have been felt — lived through as well as observed — and the recognition of this comes from the quality of the paint itself, the confidence of its handling. This is particularly true of the watercolours where the painter's fluency seems to derive not from mere facility but from his being completely ready for his subject, emotionally and technically. In such a painting as *Road between St Aubin and Benouville*, with its disparate elements of strewn camouflage screens, grounded aeroplanes, telegraph poles, Richards's conception is strong enough for him to convey information both strikingly and harmoniously. 'Once a designer, always a designer,' Richards wrote to a friend, and though the design element is submerged in his later paintings the originality and virtuosity of his designer's eye are always apparent. As a result all his war paintings have an air of strangeness, the familiar — whether battle debris, waste land, discarded equipment — viewed from an unfamiliar angle.

During the early part of the war — when he was still serving as a sapper and painting in what spare time he had — Richards wrote numerous letters in which he described in detail the pictures he was working on. Most of these were sent to the War Artists' Advisory Committee in the hope that they would like his work sufficiently to take him on. What is interesting about these letters is the emphasis they put on physical tasks — building pontoons, camouflaging camps and defence sites, erecting pill-boxes — and Richards's anxiety that all the heavy labour that had gone into these tasks should be known. It is as if he wanted to emphasise that what he was recording was an involved and arduous business.

> Bridging is the bane of a sapper's life; it is never warm on the river at night, and at 3 a.m. life in the body has ceased to exist ... A fall into the river is not the best way of starting a night's work and the bridge once started must be finished in the shortest possible time. The German sappers have found pontoon bridges a very costly business. The bridge is

built up in sections, each section being a pontoon raft. These are rowed into position and locked together to form the bridge. This is very heavy work, mainly lifting heavy girders down slippery banks onto the pontoon pier ...

It is his awareness of what such jobs involved that gives all Richards's work credibility. That he found himself so rewardingly, and with so evident a sense of self-fulfilment, in the last months of his life is some small compensation for his death.

RICHARDS, Albert, *The Road between St Aubin and Benouville*, 1944, Watercolour, $21\frac{1}{2} \times 29$ ins

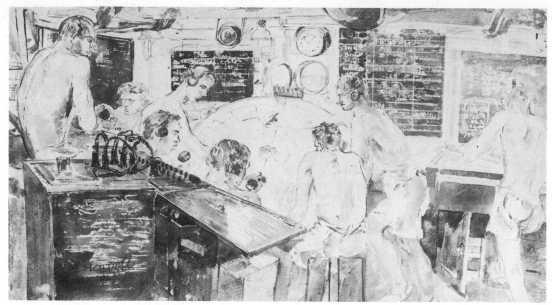

HENNELL, Thomas, *H.M.S.* Hunter *Operations Room*, 1945, Watercolour, $13\frac{5}{8} \times 25\frac{1}{8}$ ins

HENNELL, Thomas, *H.M.S.* Nelson *receiving a Japanese Vessel to make arrangements for British Occupation of Penang*, 1945, Watercolour, $18 \times 19\frac{1}{2}$ ins

# VII
# ORCHARDS TO MANGROVES

*Thomas Hennell*

You dead, my friends, still stay
Like this exquisite tree
My eyes must leave, heraldic
Flowering I will not see
Scald in April with crimson
Showers of petals. Then lie
There among its roots and blossom.
Your graces to the moonstone sky
It will yearly repay.

Bernard Gutteridge, *Gold Mohur*

War had been declared for only two months when Thomas Hennell wrote off from his home Orchard Cottage, Ridley, near Wrotham, in Kent 'Please enrol my name as an artist who wishes to make drawings as war records, whether at home or abroad. I am willing to undertake any kind of subject, whether figures, landscapes, architectural or mechanical ...'

The unassuming directness of the letter is somehow typical. Hennell was 36 at the time. His father had been Rector of Ridley and after schooling at Bradfield, study at the Regent Street Polytechnic and various teaching jobs in the west country, Thomas Hennell had returned to the Kent countryside of his childhood. It was the country of Samuel Palmer, subsequently of Graham Sutherland. In 1940, having recovered from a nervous breakdown, Hennell was doing watercolours for the Recording Britain project. He had published a book on farming and a volume of poetry.

His offer of service as a war artist was not immediately taken up. In early 1941, however, a study of land workers which Hennell had submitted to the Committee was purchased for 7 guineas. Soon afterwards they turned down a further batch of agricultural subjects and the outlook appeared unpromising.

In August, nevertheless, the Committee got in touch again with Hennell and suggested a series a watercolours on such harvest activities as threshing and baling, hedging, the clearing of orchards and so on. Hennell set off for

Hereford and Essex and, together with some made round his own home, produced seven works, all of which were accepted.

Hennell appeared to be regarded, at this stage, as some kind of charming ruralist, able to turn his hand equally to cabbages and landgirls. Indeed, his preoccupation with rustic pursuits prevented him in May of the next year from visiting the National Gallery, where his own pictures were on view, because he had to 'pack up some bees'.

These occasional agricultural commissions continued until the summer of 1943, when Hennell's fortunes took a quite different turn. He was invited in June of that year by the Ministry of Information to go to Iceland for three months on a reconnaissance mission. Ravilious had disappeared six months earlier without having time to get anything down and Hennell, though a painter of altogether quieter talent, was regarded as in the nature of a replacement.

In August 1943 Hennell was installed at the Island Hotel, Reykjavik, writing for more drawing paper. 'I am using it at the rate of a full sheet per day.' Within a month he reported that he had submitted thirty water-colours and two sketchbooks for naval censorship. They included work done at Camp Baldur 3 and on various journeys. 'If you find my drawings too peaceful and unwarlike, it is because I may only draw those things which are accessible to any civilian.'

On October 13, he wrote:

HENNELL, Thomas, *Icelandic Trawler*, Watercolour, $18\frac{3}{4} \times 24\frac{1}{8}$ ins

Akureyri was snowbound during most of my 12 days there—we had blizzards and Arctic effects. The journey home was to have been made by trawler to Seydisfiord and thence changing to another boat—but in fact the second boat's directions were changed and I waited 4 days for

another. It is a waterlogged place overhung by the mountains and I was very sorry for the Naval men who have been there in some cases for more than a year. They showed me the greatest kindness and hospitality ...

Back in England Hennell returned to his cottage in Kent, making occasional excursions north. A week in Tyneside to paint fishing boats was wasted because of bad weather. In March 1944 he wrote from Grimsby, 'I have been here since Tuesday last and find good material to draw — particularly some wooden vessels which are being built ... I have watched trawlers unloading and fish allocation.'

There were plans in May for a trip to Malta but owing to some muddle over visas this had to be shelved. On May 29 Hennell was whisked off to Portsmouth, offered a three-month commission as an honorary Lieutenant, R.N.V.R. and attached to the Press Division of the Admiralty, c/o Naval Party 1646. 'Ardizzone is here', he wrote, 'and finds subjects ready for him, but to me it is a vast, intensely complicated scene — lovely in form, light and colour.'

The scene was, of course, the final massing of the Allied armies preparatory to D-Day. On June 15, though, Hennell was observing regretfully,

> My main subjects are to be found along the beaches: they are splendid and varied, but alas! why didn't they let us come on D-Day? The doors have opened and shut and we are still in the ante-room.
>
> But indeed there are endless fine subjects — inland camps under orchards and villages with grand Norman buildings almost unscathed — the churches have got off lightly so far — the seaside villas make rather deplorable undignified wrecks.

A fortnight later Hennell was writing cheerfully that after some days under canvas he was installed in a small house along with his fellow artist, Albert Richards. 'He secludes himself daily in intense concentrations.'

The countryman in Hennell must have felt at home, for Gregory was soon writing to him, 'Your pictures [one of Caen was already hanging in the National Gallery] make me long for Normandy again. I imagine a scene with cider and cheeses predominating.'

At the end of July Hennell was back in Kent working up his sketches but anxious to get back to France. He returned to Normandy towards the end of August. 'I go to join Richards today,' he wrote on the 24th. 'We have suffered from mosquitoes and stomach ache but are still happy and well.'

On September 7 he did his best to suggest his whereabouts,

> I'm still with the Canadian unit which brought me to this town — the scene of the last act of Shaw's masterpieces. My intention is to move tomorrow to a seaport much frequented by Sickert, where I hope to make a connection with the Navy and naval subjects ... I have been quite busy ... and have made a series of groups of German (also Russian)

prisoners of war in a P.O.W. cage near my last quarters: some rounded up for search and inspection, others playing cards etc. in the enclosures. It was a motive of great interest to me ... my other new subjects include a robot-bomb launching site: some of the outfit is dismantled, but the concrete shelters, layout, rails and ramp, and the very effectual camouflage are clearly shown. To see one of these things go off must have been a terrifying experience.

While in France Hennell's commission was extended by a further three months. He left the Canadians and returned to the Navy. 'We are waiting to move into Dunkirk when it is taken.'

The autumn of 1944 was full of problems. There was no available transport and there was confusion over passes. 'I write to you in trouble', Hennell wrote to Gregory on November 15, 'for I find my work completely obstructed. One of the other war artists who was here had produced a SHAEF pass signed "By Command of General Eisenhower" ... and nothing less will now satisfy them [the Security Police].'

The weather was consistently foul and then, at the end of February 1945, Hennell had to go into hospital at Chatham for an operation. Despite all this Hennell produced a fair number of watercolours that winter, recording the Allied advance from the Normandy bridge-head into the port of Antwerp with an honest perceptiveness. Tanks, barns, bridges, foxholes; cathedrals and churches at Rouen and Calais, salvage vessels and freighters at Antwerp; barges in the harbour at Ostend; bridges and defence installations at Nijmegen. Hennell's pictures provide a kind of illustrative journal of the course of the war in north-west Europe. He was never, in the way several war artists were, particularly fascinated by the material of war. Although he conscientiously and meticulously sought out what seemed to him the most relevant subjects it was always the landscape in its seasons and the men working it that drew his sympathy. The war is never other than an intrusion; there is little glamour in Hennell's rendering of it.

Before V.E.Day there were suggestions that Hennell might be suitable to go to the Far East under the auspices of the Air Ministry. When the decision was made it was acted upon quickly. In early spring Hennell was still at work round Nijmegen, Flushing and Wemeldinge. By June 15 he was in Rangoon doing a watercolour of Lord Louis Mountbatten at a Victory Parade. In a letter from Calcutta, c/o R.A.F., P.R. Group, he sent back news of his activities. 'For the past fortnight I have been living with an RAF unit near a large airfield about 15 miles from Rangoon ... I begin to know some of the types of aircraft by sight (for the first time). The Burmese are a friendly and peaceable race. They seem to have no arts, but they can build with bamboo, pegs and wire as scientifically as our engineers with steel.'

On June 17 Hennell wrote to Sir Kenneth Clark:

I hope to make a journey shortly to a place where planes are being loaded with mules etc for the front, in company with an RAF artist named Frank Wootton. It is on Wootton's account that I am writing to you and I know that you will not grudge this intrusion on your time. Wootton is an A.C.2. and as such gets 4/– a day. He is allowed to paint in lieu of his duties as aircraftman…Could not Wootton be given commissioned rank? which he really deserves. It would save him much anxiety and enable him to work more efficiently. He is I think a really good painter with a specialist knowledge of aircraft. He was taught by Ravilious at Eastbourne.

Nothing, unfortunately for Wootton, came of this, but Hennell's rather bizarre request for one of his own painting umbrellas to be flown out to him met with success.

By early August Hennell had twice recovered from bouts of dysentery and managed to send back seventeen drawings rolled up in pieces of bamboo. 'I had a good fortnight at Pegu and am off to Kandy to recuperate.' The drawings were mainly to do with the laying of foundations for an airstrip by Indian troops at Pegu, but there were also watercolours of sampans on the Rangoon river and other exotic features of Burmese life.

HENNELL, Thomas,
*R.N. Camp Baldur 3:
Handling Depth Charges,*
Watercolour,
$11\frac{1}{2} \times 18\frac{5}{8}$ins

In September Hennell was in Singapore, from where he sent home another fourteen drawings. 'The best two are, I think, the operations room of H.M.S. *Hunter* and the P.O.W.s—Dodds got me a passage from Ceylon to Penang, on the Hunter and thence I came here by flying boat.'

'There is much to do', he went on, '— indeed I have many sketches — including one of Admiral Walker signing up the Penang settlement with the Jap admiral. I expect to visit Java—and there perhaps we shall see horrors, for I hear the internment camps are very bad. I am very fit and willing to go on as long as the committee wishes.'

Java was reached towards the end of October. 'I am now at Soerabaya (east end of Java) where it is difficult to receive mail; but I shall return to Singapore: meanwhile am concerned to know whether your committee wish me either (i) to return to England immediately via India or (ii) to "cover" Hong-kong, Borneo, Tokyo and to return to U.K. via Australia. I shan't try to send you any drawings at least till I get back to Singapore and if I return direct I shall carry them with me.'

That was the last anyone heard from Hennell. On November 11 Blackborow of the Air Ministry wrote to Gregory, 'I have now received further news regarding Hennell, although there is, I am afraid, nothing definite. It appears that he was last seen on Monday 5th November with a Sten Gun in Surabaya Hotel where there was trouble with the Indonese. He became separated from the other members of the party and has not been seen since. This information was brought back by a War Correspondent who returned to Singapore last Thursday.'

It was a far cry from Hennell's modest drawings of Kentish harvests and farm workers to his last works in Burma. On the way he had gone north to Iceland and followed the Allied armies in their long trek from the beaches of Normandy to the German frontier. Few, if any other, war artists experienced such varied battle fronts. The scale of Hennell's art remained modest but he was always able to respond, intuitively and sympathetically, to whatever situation he was in. His pictures relate to the aftermath of battle rather than to battle itself. But in painting sideshows Hennell remained faithful to his practical country origins; the work in his pictures—building huts, sifting rubble, unloading flour, loading parcels—is respected for what it is. His art had little time to ripen in the sun of India and Burma, and the talent that was finally extinguished in Java was a peculiarly English one. But in keeping with this, Hennell's watercolours of Iceland and north-western Europe vouchsafe for specific incidents in identifiable kinds of weather. Their low-key response to variables of climate indicate a determination to get both the mood and the setting right.

HENNELL, Thomas, *Troops going ashore over a Pontoon, Normandy*, 1944,
Watercolour, $17\frac{3}{8} \times 22$ ins

HENNELL, Thomas, *U.S. Gun Station 'Rocky Point' Hvitanes*, 1943,
Watercolour, $10\frac{1}{8} \times 18\frac{5}{8}$ ins

# VIII
# HOME FRONT

*Keith Vaughan, William Scott,*
*Rodrigo Moynihan*

All day it has rained, and we on the edge of the moors
Have sprawled in our bell tents, moody and dull as boors,
Groundsheets and blankets spread on the muddy ground
And from the first grey wakening we have found
No refuge from the skirmishing fine rain
And the wind that made the canvas heave and flap
And the taut wet guy-ropes ravel out and snap.

Alun Lewis, *All Day It Has Rained*

## Keith Vaughan

Although painters of completely different impulse, Keith Vaughan and
William Scott were almost exactly of an age. Moreover they had enough
in common to share, in 1946, a touring exhibition with John Minton and
Michael Ayrton. In terms of the war they were odd men out, painters
scarcely started on their careers, for whom the war simply meant defer-
ment and frustration. For neither of them did the war produce those
incidental rewards—human and artistic—which came the way of many
artists obliged to do work and live lives they would not otherwise have
done. Yet in neither case were their years of war service totally wasted.
Scott, who served in the Royal Engineers from 1942–6, produced a
number of oils and watercolours which, though they seem to have meant
little to him at the time, nevertheless survive as evidence of reluctant
attachment to a romantic manner. Vaughan, who served as a non-com-
batant in the Pioneer Corps, made numerous drawings of barrack life and
of his fellow soldiers. These, especially where they concern the human
figure, relate more to the themes and obsessions of his subsequent career
than anything in Scott's war pictures. The work of both conveys something of the sense of loss and displacement that was common to civilians in
uniform. They were in the war but scarcely of it, in Vaughan's case by
precariously held convictions.

Immediately war was declared Vaughan joined the St John's Ambulance. On November 15 he described in his journal the kind of day typical of military life for most soldiers most of the time.

> Nothing is demanded from me but inaction and acceptance of mild discomforts. The hours of my waking and sleeping are fixed...We continue to play games. Ping-pong, billiards, and first-aid, bending intimately over each other and feeling for arteries and pressure points through thick clothing. Tying each other up with splints and bandages.
>
> There is warmth and toleration in my associates. If there is not friendliness it is only because of my own awkwardness and inability to share my life with theirs. I envy the ordered simplicity of their lives, but I remain a spectator and never a participant.

That feeling, despite his inward craving for a total relationship, always remained true for Vaughan. His barrack-room sketches convey, in their simplicity of line, a genial sense of camaraderie but the journal entries of the war years more frequently suggest loneliness. 'I feel myself being pushed further and further towards the very edge of life beyond which lies total isolation.'

VAUGHAN, Keith,
*A Barrack Room — Sleep*,
Watercolour,
$9\frac{5}{8} \times 12\frac{7}{8}$ ins

It was typical of Vaughan that he should worry away incessantly over matters of principle. Yet 'it is more my reason that is offended by this war than my conscience.'

In June 1940 he was among those receiving and attending to the wounded returning from Dunkirk, Germans among them. 'We worked on through the night, through each intimate and infinite tragedy, not noticing when it turned to day. Above the last stretcher the sky was already blue and adorned with morning. The doctors made a last round of the ambulances, checking forms, adding signatures—final instructions. The train lay behind us, a hollow, picked carcase, the whiteness of the carriages now grey and dirty in the morning light.'

It is plain from the quality of Vaughan's diary observations that, in different circumstances, he could have been an outstanding war artist. He was, for example, one of the very few painters of the time primarily concerned with the human figure. Under a dry, reserved exterior he was passionate, amusing and caring, at the same time totally unsentimental. Had he been obliged to share fully in the lives of soldiers at the front he might have been able to involve himself as a painter in more challenging ways. As it is, his drawings of soldiers in camp and German prisoners of war have a quality of ironic compassion, conveying the sense of enforced idleness and relaxation from hard physical labour that soldiers lounging about in their billets usually exude.

In June 1940, Vaughan's younger brother Dick—a pilot in the R.A.F.—was killed. In August Vaughan attended a Conscientious Objectors tribunal at Reading and was recommended for service with the R.A.M.C. He hoped at one moment that he would be given a job in camouflage, but in the end it was the Pioneer Corps to which, on January 2, 1941, he was called up.

His first summer was spent in camps at Bulford, Codford and Melksham, working on the land, quarrying gravel. Surprisingly, he soon settled down in his platoon of individuals and eccentrics. 'There are days when I feel more alive, vigorous and happy than I can ever remember. If only one had more time and leisure and the work were not so physically exhausting.'

Soon however the repetition and pointlessness of the routine, the constant breaking up of units and transfer of friends, resulted in such feelings of futility that joining a combatant unit began to seem preferable. The Germans were already fighting on Russian soil, the Battle of Britain had been fought and won, the Blitz was in full swing.

A profound and moving confidence in human relationships emerges from both journal entries and drawings. The faces of soldiers seem incredibly youthful, touching in their vulnerability and apparent innocence. After spending a whole morning painting a Nissen hut Vaughan records in his journal how he got up to stretch his back and saw a boy ride by on a bicycle. 'If one could sustain the welded sensations of that complex moment throughout the time necessary for painting, one might succeed in painting the subject of a boy on a bicycle.'

He may not have done that, but Vaughan's drawings illuminate many aspects of similar physical intimacy — men smoking and playing cards, reading letters on their bunks, most often simply resting. It is not the most dashing or glamorous side of military life, but probably it is the most real.

However, being Vaughan, he soon began to question the validity of war-time relationships. 'Under all the conditions of war men are something less than their true selves, are artificially confined to a pattern of intense stimulus, fear, anxiety, strain. It is through these conditions commonly shared that one imagines oneself at one with them, but it is an illusion. Remove the conditions and the bond vanishes.'

Vaughan wrote with some insight on the attractions of service life, as exemplified by Richard Hillary and T.E. Lawrence. 'The support that banishes the fear of freedom. It gives pilots their strange, strained, rather hectic dignity,' what Hillary called the 'ethereal' quality. 'It is the reason why so many people are really happier during a war than in peace time. They are given an artificial armour over their soft shells.'

On May 1, 1943 Vaughan wrote in his diary: 'The prime concern of the artist is not to urge the course of events in one direction or another but to understand what is going on, record it, and resolve the conflict in terms of his art ... Ultimately it is his imaginative comprehension that counts.'

VAUGHAN, Keith,
*A Barrack Room*, 1942,
Watercolour,
$8\frac{7}{8} \times 11\frac{1}{2}$ ins

In July Vaughan travelled north to Yorkshire and for most of the rest of the war worked at a German prisoner-of-war camp. 'The war has divided us into two species between which there is hardly any means of communication; those who have been caught up in the destruction and those who have escaped.'

He was demobilised on March 16, 1946. 'Rapid disintegration of personality. Integrity melting like ice in the sun.' As a painter he was involved only with the victims of war, not the heroes; with those whose needs and loneliness and desire for reassurance he understood. The soldiers in his drawings have no weapons, no rank; they are simply themselves.

Thirty years later, suffering from cancer, Vaughan committed suicide. The gentle drawings of the war years, with their emphasis on involuntary, shared situations, had given way to powerful semi-abstract landscapes in which men, stripped to essentials, struggled to free themselves from their natural bonds. Vaughan's art was essentially erotic and uncompromising, though beneath its austerity of vision there lay the same hankerings for romantic fulfilment that had characterised his earliest drawings. If anyone painted brotherly love it was he.

FURSE, Roger,
*A Studious Sailor*,
Watercolour, 19⅝ × 13 ins

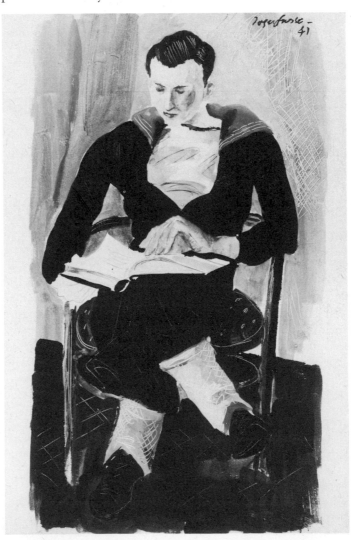

# William Scott

A barn is not called a barn, to put it more plainly,
Or a field in the distance, where sheep may be safely grazing.
You must never be over-sure. You must say, when reporting:
At five o'clock in the central sector is a dozen
Of what appear to be animals; whatever you do,
    Don't call the bleeders *sheep*.

             Henry Reed, *Judging Distances*

The subject matter of William Scott's war paintings was in many ways similar to Vaughan's: soldiers sleeping and writing letters, prisoner-of-war camps, camouflaged lorries, night convoys. 'While in the Army,' Scott remarked in a 1972 interview with Alan Bowness, 'I painted some water-colour landscapes but felt that these paintings, done in very difficult conditions, were not really a continuation of what I had started in Brittany. I was caught up in a wave of the English watercolour nationalist, romantic patriotic isolationist self-preservationist movement.'

  Scott's war-time pictures were essentially illustrative and anecdotal, not dissimilar in manner to John Minton's paintings of the time. As such they stand isolated from the rest of his work, which has always been con-cerned — whether its ostensible subject matter has been kitchen utensils or the female nude — with formal problems, proportion, space, colour. The object, in a recognisable, associative form, became increasingly ambiguous in Scott's work, so it is scarcely surprising that the paintings of his army years came to seem untypically direct to him. Most artists, in whatever medium, want to feel that their work is all of a piece. What

SCOTT, William,
*Interior with Soldiers*,
Watercolour, $5\frac{5}{8} \times 7\frac{5}{8}$ ins

paintings Scott did during the war were in a prevailing style, rather than his own.

Whatever experiences they had in common during the war Scott and Vaughan could scarcely have had more dissimilar private lives. Where Vaughan was solitary and homosexual, Scott had married in 1937 a fellow student and settled in Brittany, where they started a summer painting school. Scott, despite doubts about whether it was the right road for him, worked on landscapes rather in the manner of Cezanne. In due course he realised his mistake. 'I don't respond to air and sea and the things of nature,' he said to Alan Bowness, 'and when I approached landscape it was the man-made things that attracted me. In any case I had already discovered that my real love was the still life.'

When war broke out the Scotts moved to Dublin, then London, and finally Somerset. At Bath Academy of Art Scott did some part-time teaching, at the same time getting work ready for a one-man show at the Leger Galleries. Due to be called up, he volunteered in June 1942 for the Navy but was rejected. The Army, however, took him and he was drafted into the R.A.O.C. Luckily, he was stationed initially in London so was free to use his old Chelsea studio in his spare time. It was here, during the winter of 1942–3, that he painted *Soldier and Girl Sleeping*, shown at the Leicester Gallery's 'Artists of Fame and Promise' show in February. About this he wrote: 'You saw people asleep everywhere. It was one of the things about

Scott, William,
*Camouflaged Soldiers*,
Gouache, $6\frac{1}{4} \times 13\frac{1}{4}$ ins

the war. It was like a kind of neurosis. Young soldiers especially were constantly asleep ... ' His duty hours involved him in the less exacting task of whitewashing walls.

In due course, partly, it seems, because of the intervention of Sir Kenneth Clark, Scott was transferred to the Ordnance Section at Ruabon in North Wales. In the more congenial atmosphere of map-makers Scott was happier, though still lonely. In London he had painted, as well as *Soldier and Girl Sleeping*, two similarly-sized oils on war subjects: *Night Convoy* and *Camouflaged Soldier*. At Ruabon he produced seventy watercolours, mostly of soldiers in Welsh settings. These were shown in 1945 at the Leger Galleries, but no more than half a dozen have since been traced. Here, too, Scott did the illustrations for the anthology, *Soldiers' Verse*, edited by W.J. Turner and Sheila Shannon.

Of all Scott's war pictures *Soldier and Girl Sleeping* and *Night Convoy* remain the most effective. In general, his view of warfare was the reverse of romantic or heroic. 'We were always driving somewhere, we were never told where and it was always night.' This feeling of futility, of being helplessly in the hands of others, was one common to all soldiers away from the front. News was sketchy, often false; rumours proliferated. Troops were kept busy by being sent on routine manoeuvres or by being set trivial tasks. Scott was lucky in that he was in decent countryside and able to paint. But, as he remarked to Alan Bowness, 'I felt terribly lonely. During those years when I was in the army there was a tremendous amount of discussion and talk about the English Romantic landscape painters, and this was a tradition I did not belong to. It was not my kind of painting at all.'

Yet, awkward for him though the idiom of *Soldier and Girl Sleeping* and

*Night Convoy* may have been, in their suggestions of fatigue and alienation these are paintings true to their time. Painters like Scott, mere cogs in the military machine, may in many ways have been nearer to civilians than to servicemen. But if they could not be articulate about the conditions and feelings of the fighting soldier, they shared his loss of freedom, his separation from family and friends. *Soldier and Girl Sleeping* evokes, as well as fatigue, the need for human contact, for the touch of flesh. *Night Convoy* with its diminishing perspective of blind, barrack-like buildings, its figures loaded like refuse into trucks going from nowhere to nowhere, is a parable of nightmare. These are flat paintings but their very flatness contributes to their effect.

In January 1946 Scott was demobilised, returning at once to his job at Bath. He has made little subsequent reference to his work of the war years, and indeed, in any consideration of his career as a painter, it looks oddly, both stylistically and in terms of subject matter. But however grudgingly, he made his mark.

SCOTT, William, *Night Convoy*, Gouache, $5\frac{1}{4} \times 7\frac{5}{8}$ ins

# Rodrigo Moynihan

This is a damned unnatural sort of war;
The pilots sits among the clouds quite sure
About the values he is fighting for;
He cannot hear beyond the veil of sound.

He cannot see the people on the ground;
He only knows that on the sloping map
Of sea-fringed town and country people creep
Like ants—and who cares if ants laugh or weep?

R.N. Currey, *Disintegration of Springtime*

Rodrigo Moynihan, a few years older than Scott and Vaughan, had even less of a fulfilling war. He spent a wretched two years as a private soldier in a Signal Training regiment; had no sooner been transferred to a camouflage unit, than he had a breakdown; finally, appointed an official war artist in a civilian capacity, had to spend much of his time waiting for senior officers to find time to sit. Nevertheless, Moynihan's dozen or so pictures of the time contain at least two, his portrait of an A.T.S. private, and his group undergoing Medical Inspection, that vividly encapsulate their subjects.

Although only 29 at the outbreak of war Moynihan had already been through several phases as a painter. In 1932–3 he had been a member of the London Group, a year later of the Objective Abstraction Group. By 1937 he was painting in the manner of the Euston Road school.

It was not surprising, therefore, that Moynihan should have been approached by the Ministry of Information in July 1940. Their initial proposal was that he should produce two paintings on R.A.F. subjects. Accordingly, Moynihan established himself at the George Hotel, Huntingdon, where by the end of the summer he had finished studies of a Vickers-Wellington AC1 Bomber and of two Blenheim bombers.

In October Moynihan received his call-up papers and was sent first to Colchester, then to Whalley in Lancashire for signal training. From here he wrote in November to the War Artists' Advisory Committee, inquiring about the possibility of transferring to Camouflage, a process that had to be initiated through Moynihan's C.O. 'I find I am in a highly specialised section and have misgivings on my ability to cope with the Morse Code and the insides of motor cycles. The course takes six months and although I feel I can manage three of them, can't see how I can manage the rest.'

He continued, 'I have had no opportunity or inclination to paint yet. There are plenty of subjects—but I feel too much like the apple in the still-life. Hardly detached enough.'

During the next few months efforts were made, by Sir Kenneth Clark and Sir Edward Marsh among others, to improve Moynihan's situation. For one reason or another they came to nothing. Moynihan managed to paint an occasional picture, the Committee purchasing his *Three Soldiers off* to *O.C.T.U.* in July. But in August he was writing very dispiritedly from Preston. 'My enthusiasm, I must confess, is somewhat gone after all these endless months. The red-tape obstructionism and rank injustice of the system is a revelation. In addition, I have a feeling of personal humiliation which it will take me a long time to forget.'

Moynihan appears to have taken his failure to get a transfer to Camouflage exceptionally hard. From the correspondence available the reason for this failure seems to have been the belief that, as one Colonel put it, 'artists make good soldiers' and that therefore Moynihan was better off where he was.

By late November he was in the Shetlands. 'It is fairly bleak here, though there is a splendid mixture of sea, loch and mountain which I would like to paint. But my existence is pointless at the moment.'

He was able, nevertheless, to make the odd trip to London, though an expedition to see his work in a show of war art at the National Gallery was not entirely successful. 'I was sorry not to have arrived in time for the ceremonial opening of the new room at the N.G. I stupidly mixed up the times and when I arrived Stanley Spencer and a semi-intoxicated Keeper were the only occupants.'

This period was the lowest point in Moynihan's war. In April 1942 the transfer was unexpectedly achieved and Moynihan was able to write to Dickey from Farnham. 'I have finally been commissioned and am now in camouflage. The dragon gave one final twist but last week was completely overcome. After all your efforts—and my pleadings—I am really full of gratitude.'

MOYNIHAN, Rodrigo,
*Medical Inspection*, 1943,
Oil, 36 × 48 ins

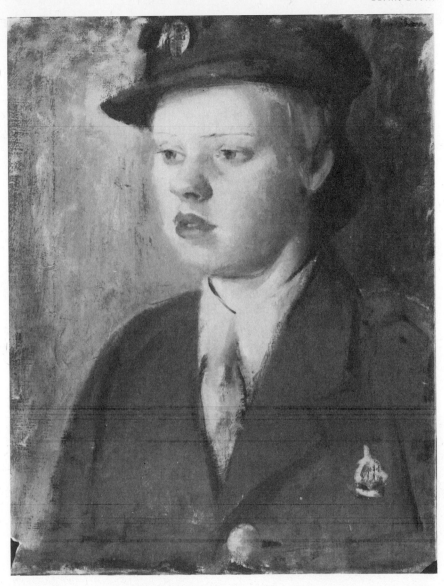

MOYNIHAN, Rodrigo,
*Private Clark, A.T.S.*, Oil,
18 × 14 ins

It was not long, however, before Moynihan's health broke down and he was invalided out of the army. Things looked up again when, in July 1943, he was appointed a war artist in a civilian capacity. Over the next year he painted, as well as the pictures already mentioned, numerous portraits, among them a Regimental Sergeant Major in the A.T.S., two Lieutenant-Generals, a Major-General, an Admiral, an Air Marshal, and the two scientists, Sir George Thomson and Professor J.D. Cockcroft. All Moynihan's portraits combine likeness with a sense of personality, though his war-time commissioned work is understandably blander than some of

*opposite,*
HENDERSON, Keith, *An Air Gunner in a Gun Turret* (detail), Oil, 30 × 40ins

*overleaf, above left,*
COLDSTREAM, Sir William, *Rifleman Mangal Singh,* Oil, 24 × 19ins

*overleaf, above right,*
ROSOMAN, LEONARD, *A Range-Finder in Hot Sunlight,* Oil, 20 × 16ins

*overleaf, below,*
MOYNIHAN, Rodrigo, *Two Blenheims,* Oil, 30 × 25ins

his later portraits of friends such as William Coldstream and Francis Bacon.

*Medical Inspection* is another matter altogether. Moynihan has always shown particular skill in the relating of figures in a group and in this study of several half-undressed men some of the sense of indignity and humiliation he had himself felt comes across. The stooped men, with their white depressed flesh, their awkwardness in the presence of a medical officer, are turned into archetypal figures. It is the onlooker who feels the embarrassment and indignity of the situation rather than the soldiers who, in their fumbling fashion, simply accept what they have to do. But Moynihan has managed to express by the painting of postures military subservience, the reduction of individuals to mere numbers, official indifference.

*Private Clark,* on the other hand, is painted with Pasmore-like lushness. She is not a beauty, but her red lips, her youthful freshness and glowing skin, the sense of a concealed sensuality, are all, in contrast to the rough, commonplace uniform, wonderfully appealing. This is the sort of image of which the dreams of ordinary soldiers, removed from their own women, are made. She is the girl they would like to take to the troop concert or come across in the NAAFI. The effectiveness of Moynihan's painting derives partly from the fact that girls like Private Clark, however inaccessible they might have been, had the look of availability, the common touch.

BONE, Stephen, *The Shadow of a Kite Balloon,* Oil, 9¾ × 13½ ins

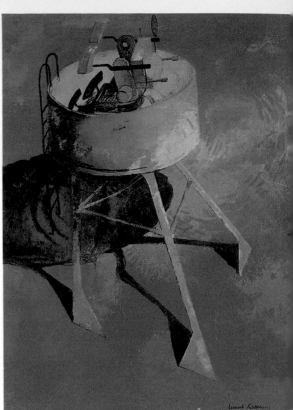

# IX
# AFRICA AND BEYOND

*Edward Ardizzone, Edward Bawden,*
*Anthony Gross, William Coldstream*

Green, green is El Aghir. It has a railway-station,
And the wealth of its soil has borne another fruit,
A mairie, a school and an elegant Salle de Fêtes.
Such blessings, as I remarked, in effect, to the waiter,
Are added unto them that have plenty of water.

Norman Cameron, Green, Green is El Aghir

## Edward Ardizzone

In December 1939 Edward Ardizzone was a Bombadier attached to F
Troop, 162 Anti-Aircraft Battery, Royal Artillery, Woolwich. He was the
same age as the century, having been born in 1900 in Indo-China of Italian
and Scottish parents. At the time of his call-up he was known mainly for
his bibulous watercolours of urban life—bars, cafés, theatres, pubs, prosti-
tutes, cyclists—and as a writer and illustrator of children's books. The idea
of war in relation to the convivial nature of Ardizzone's art, with its plump
figures and curvaceous lines, is faintly incongruous. But in fact, once he
had ceased to be, in his own words, 'a rather inefficient officer in the mud of
a gunsite in South London', and had become an official war artist, he
became one of the most prolific and travelled of all of them. In 1940 he was
sent to France and Belgium before being evacuated three months later with
the B.E.F. from Boulogne. During the next two years he was in London
doing drawings of the Blitz, as well as of the Home Guard and military life
in Northern Ireland and the West Country. In 1942 he sailed in the wake of
the 8th Army to the Western Desert via South Africa, subsequently
following the liberating armies to Sicily and up the coast of Italy as far as
Florence. He returned to Britain in time to set off for Normandy shortly
after D-Day. He was back in Italy during the winter of 1944–5, travelling
to Germany and Denmark before being demobilised in May 1945.

During all this time Ardizzone produced several hundred drawings and
watercolours, as well as an illustrated journal, parts of which were later
published in *Baggage to the Enemy*, the account of his experiences in 1940,

*opposite,*
McGRATH, Raymond,
*Hangars,* 1940, Water-
colour, $14\frac{3}{4} \times 21\frac{1}{2}$ ins

*overleaf,*
NEVINSON, C.R.W.,
*Anti-Aircraft Defences,* Oil,
$32 \times 24$ ins

ARDIZZONE, Edward, *The Barmaid at the Red Lion*, Watercolour, $9\frac{5}{8} \times 9\frac{1}{4}$ ins

and in his *Diary of a War Artist*. The drawings are of varying quality, mostly done in great haste and difficult conditions, but seen as individual pages have liveliness and charm. 'A maddening war,' Ardizzone observed, 'only the dead and the dying stay still for you to draw.'

It would have been unrealistic to have expected anything bitter, sharply satiric or even moving from Ardizzone. His art, anecdotal, affectionate, nostalgic, works best when subject and style relate, that is to say in his studies of cosy saloon bars or officers' messes, inside canteens or interiors of barracks—situations when he was able to isolate idiosyncratic gestures and attitudes and record architectural details. The people in these pictures—boozy colonels or awkward and exhausted other ranks—have an expressiveness and immediacy that suggest non-existent captions. They seem to be speaking; imaginary dialogue is in the air.

Ardizzone was least at home in the desert in 1942; the vast distances, lack of perspective and dramatic feature, made it hard for him to give his groups of soldiers and equipment the intimacy his kind of art needed. From all other subjects—the Blitz, Home Guard activities, France, the advance north from Italy—there were pictorial rewards, though usually of a fairly comic sort. Military life, when not tragic or boring, is memorable mainly for its comic aspects. Ardizzone, if unable to suggest adequately the tragedy or the tedium, managed to convey the entertainment.

One of his best-known watercolours *Priest Begging a Lift*, done in Louvain in 1940, demonstrates how, unconsciously, Ardizzone turns what must have been in reality a desperate situation into something approaching farce. The portly priest, entreating transport in a town probably soon to be captured, seems more like someone singing an aria than a man at the end of his tether. What Ardizzone has drawn is probably exactly what he saw; another artist would have seen it differently. The earthiness of Ardizzone's temperament enabled him to defuse the tensions of warfare. In this respect, on the level at which he operates, his vision approximated to that of the average civilian in uniform.

Another of his most popular works *A Battle in an Orchard of Almond Trees*, made in Italy in 1943, exposes Ardizzone's limitations. Gabriel White, in his book, *Edward Ardizzone*, describes it as 'his most vivid depiction of warfare and its bitter wastage of human life, in a sense the climax of his work as a war artist ... where tragedy is contrasted with the wild beauty of the scene.'

It is, certainly, a very pretty watercolour, but despite the exhausted soldiers by the roadside, the corpses and stray boots and loose wheels, it is the prettiness of the scene, not the tragedy, that Ardizzone makes one aware of. He is incapable of a bitter line. The corpses, differently captioned, could almost be drunks fallen off a lorry after a party. Almost. In fact, just as Ardizzone usually stops short in his drawings of caricature, so in this

ARDIZZONE, Edward, *The General of an Armoured Division sitting beside his Tank*, Watercolour, $7\frac{1}{8} \times 10$ ins

ARDIZZONE, Edward,
*Difficulties of the Language*,
Watercolour, $6\frac{1}{4} \times 8\frac{1}{4}$ins

picture the presence of tanks, the glimpse of soldiers moving through the
almond trees in the background, give a certain credibility to the illusion of
battle. Probably in this watercolour Ardizzone came as near as he ever did
to suggesting the shambles and human loss of a real action, involving actual
men, but his idiom is against him. It would be unfair to describe it as a
landscape with some dead thrown in for effect, because plainly Ardizzone
is at pains to contrast the beauty of the trees with the blindness of the
soldiers, dead or alive, to their surroundings. But Ardizzone fails to effect
the pictorial reconciliation, or integration, of two disparate elements.
What set him off usually were the characteristic poses of people unobserved
at recreation. In this instance he was faced with pictorial problems related
to subject matter and while he could solve them on a purely visual level, on
the level of feeling his familiar technique was inadequate.

In his *Diary of a War Artist*, which begins with the invasion of Sicily,
Ardizzone describes how, initially, his method was to make pencil jottings
in a tiny notebook, then return to base and work them up into watercolours. When he was in Cairo he bought a larger notebook and used ink,
these later illustrations to journal entries being more realised as well as
more permanent. The drawings, though aids to memory in the first
instance, are often engaging in their own right.

The diary itself makes for strange reading. The realities of war certainly
intrude but when they do Ardizzone treats them in such matter-of-fact
fashion that death often seems a mere footnote to some glorious jaunt. On
July 16, 1943 he writes: 'I do some drawings and have a snooze. We drink a
bottle of Ronnie's champagne. Heaven. Brought to earth by the smell of
dead bodies hidden somewhere, a smell that haunts one everywhere. Head
back for Syracuse, pass an open lorry of Italian prisoners in civilian dress, a

dejected lot. The MP in charge told us they were paratroops caught wearing civilian dress, they will probably be shot. I think by the look of them they realized that too.'

A day later he is writing:

> The fowl marvellous. We drink champagne and eat grapes. It is a feast …The approach to the bridge was a chaos of burnt-out Bren gun carriers, tanks and 88s. Across the bridge and to the left a ruined farmhouse and vinery. Where the road turned it ran along a wide ditch. In the ditch the appalling remains of many German dead. Bodies disembowelled, stripped of their clothes, blackened legs and arms gone, and even one fearful cadaver blown in half.
>
> A trio of smells. The terrible smell of the dead, the smell of roasting bodies from two of our tanks shattered and burnt out beside an 88, and the heavy smell of new wine from the winery.
>
> We meet a weary Colonel and his Captain and offer them champagne.

There are many vivid descriptions in the journals of landscape, of comic incidents and good open-air meals, of rough travel and what Ardizzone calls 'usual front line horrors'. For example, 'A man squashed by a tank, many dead and the macabre effect of an artificial leg lying among the dead by the roadside.'

In Italy Ardizzone came into his own, choosing his own activities and sometimes coming under fire. He wandered about by himself, sometimes

ARDIZZONE, Edward, *Staff Officers*, Watercolour, $9\frac{5}{8} \times 10\frac{3}{4}$ ins

on a bicycle, not always sure where he or the enemy were. He made drawings of troops sunning themselves or round fires in bitter cold, of blossom coming out in the valleys and of snow in the mountains, of blown bridges and discarded machinery. He conveys excellently the sense of movement in campaigning, the disorder.

It was not in Ardizzone's nature to analyse or reflect. He had a healthy feeling for material comfort, for the pleasures of the table. He got by as best he could, using his wits to serve both himself and his art. He was obliged to witness much that was horrible and depressing, but having recorded it in as detached a fashion as possible he hurries on to pleasanter matters. He never lost his zest for new places and experiences, a delight in weather, an exhilaration in arrival and departure. On occasions he can seem superficial and frivolous, but he is never false or hypocritical. He understood as well as anyone what he could and could not do.

At various times, especially in the Middle East, Ardizzone met up with other war artists and war correspondents, among the former, Barnett Freedman, Edward Bawden, Anthony Gross and William Coldstream. Of these, Bawden and Gross were closest in experience to Ardizzone and it was as eventual replacement for Bawden that Ardizzone was originally posted to North Africa. Ardizzone wrote to Sir Kenneth Clark about the prospect of this on March 18, 1942: 'The excitement of seeing something new and the additional income (very important with a growing family) have helped very much to decide me…I have felt for some time I was getting stale and perhaps a new scene will give me the right kick like Delacroix and Algeria, though I have no right to make a parallel between such an artist and myself.'

HAYES, Colin, *An Italian Medium Tank*, 1942, Watercolour, $9 \times 13\frac{1}{2}$ ins

# Edward Bawden

Aniseed has a sinful taste:
at your elbow a woman's voice
like, I imagine, the voice of ghosts,
demanding food. She has no grace

but, diseased and blind of an eye
and heavy with habitual dolour,
listlessly finds you and I
and the table are the same colour.

Keith Douglas, *Egypt*

The eighty-eight letters Edward Bawden wrote to his wife, and which he presented to the Imperial War Museum, provide, next to Ardizzone's diaries, the fullest account of any war artist's experiences. They range from two to eight pages in length, all meticulously written in a sloping spiky, calligrapher's hand, with scarcely a crossing out. Curiously reserved, almost impersonal in tone, they describe journeys, meals, billets, land-scapes, and a good many illnesses. At their best, they offer neat character sketches and amusing gossip.

It was in March 1940 at Arras that Bawden first came across Ardizzone. They were sharing a house when Ardizzone was suddenly struck down with excruciating lumbago. He had to be carried to bed, but no sooner was he manoeuvred there with great difficulty than he wanted to get up again and go to the bathroom. This he was unable to do, so Bawden had to hold a jerry for him.

Bawden was impressed with Ardizzone's swift recovery and immediate re-kindling of appetites, as well as his ability to see that they lived on the best available. About Anthony Gross, whom he met in Egypt and got on well with, Bawden wrote, 'I like his work a great deal; fresh observation and quiet humour; unpretentious and good; the school of Ardizzone and Topolski—the sound tradition of English draughtsmanship and illustration which harks back to Rowlandson and Bunbury, don't you agree?'

It was not until November 1944 that Bawden met Coldstream, then on a visit to Rome from Pisa to consult a doctor about an abscess on the arm.

At tea this afternoon Coldstream gave a wicked imitation of a prayer-meeting led by Herbert Read and Ben and Barbara praying with Salvation Army gusto, confessing their sins of representation, and asking the good Lord to make them abstract and advanced … Cold-stream accepts as an axiom that, though one may wish to change oneself and to make the effort from time to time is salutory, yet one is driven back upon the way one is accustomed to paint, from which there is no real or easy escape.

BAWDEN, Edward,
*A Midland Battalion at*
*Mersa Matruh*,
Watercolour,
$11\frac{1}{4} \times 35\frac{3}{4}$ ins

Osbert Lancaster makes an appearance in Rome a few months later, on leave from Greece. 'His trim Edwardian figure of an immaculate dandy and flamboyant whiskers did not look out of place in an ornate Roman setting; he stepped daintily like an old tom, stealthily, cat-like towards me on the rich red carpet. "Athens is right up your street — but I shall be seeing you there shortly."'

Bawden's letters, though lacking in intimacy, nevertheless enable one to chart his movements with accuracy. They provide, too, a useful background to his drawings.

Having parted from Ardizzone after the evacuation from France, during which Bawden made several hasty but atmospheric drawings from Dunkirk, he left England in July for North Africa. This involved a sea voyage to Cape Town, a rail journey from there to Durban and finally a flight to Cairo.

Within two months he was on his way to Khartoum by paddle steamer and train. This was the beginning of a series of painting forays that took Bawden to Roseires, Gubba, Addis Ababa, Asmara, Siwa Oasis, the Western Desert, the Lebanon, Iraq and Saudi Arabia. After two years abroad he set sail for home on the S.S. *Laconia*, having joined her at Cape Town. They were torpedoed 600 miles from Lagos, and after five days in a lifeboat survivors were picked up by the Vichy warship *La Gloire* and taken to Casablanca for internment. From this Bawden was rescued by the arrival of the Americans. He was taken to Norfolk, Virginia, arriving home in a convoy early in 1943.

The rest of that spring and summer Bawden was at home in East Anglia in Colchester Military Hospital with a skin complaint, recovering from which he spent some weeks with parachute regiments in Scotland.

By September, however, he was off again, first to Cairo and then to Baghdad, where he spent the best part of a year. He was back in Rome for Christmas 1944, was at Boulogne when Berlin fell, and at Udine on V.E. Day. In the heat of July he was down in Naples, where Coldstream and he joined forces and spent most of their nights killing bed-bugs.

Among Bawden's letters, three, in their different ways, are of particular interest. On October 16, 1941, he wrote to Dickey from Cairo, remarking that it was an incontrovertible fact that no good painting had ever been done of Africa: 'It does seem almost impossible to find means to represent the intensity of the light, and in this connexion it is interesting to note that photographs taken in the sun-glare of the desert give the effect of the diffused light of a grey day.'

He goes on in the same letter,

The high altitude of Ethiopia and Eritrea produced unpleasant nervous systems of which I did not realize the cause until I descended to the lower levels of the Sudan and Egypt. Throughout almost the whole time spent at a high altitude I felt unwell, which necessarily controlled the amount of work I had hoped to do. On the other hand the loveliness of the Ethiopian countryside, the lush green valleys, the bare mountain passes, was immensely attractive …

It often seemed to me unfair that I should enjoy the privilege of remaining an official War Artist in the Middle East when there are so many competent painters at home … If you decided to withdraw my appointment in order that I could join the Forces as an ordinary soldier I should consider it fair treatment; so many others have not had the privilege of being able to pursue their civilian occupations. I must admit that I thoroughly enjoy the life, that trekking and camping or a long march gives immense pleasure.

There was not much likelihood of Bawden's offer being taken up, both on grounds of health and age (he was forty), but it is a decent and generous gesture all the same.

On July 26, 1942, he wrote to his wife, 'I am afraid I shall be a prize bore whenever I return. A solitary life for two years no doubt wrought a change. I have adapted myself to new interests and lost temporarily some of the old ones. The people I want to see can almost be counted on one hand.' It is ironic that, apart from immediate family, the only two names he mentions, Eric Ravilious and Tom Hennell, were to die as war artists, Ravilious within a few months, Hennell three years later.

There was a possibility early in 1944 of arrangements being made for Bawden to visit China. Nothing came of them, but while it still seemed likely Bawden wrote to Gregory from Baghdad. He was plainly excited by the idea but his description of the life he thought he was leaving vividly complements his drawings of the period.

> I shall feel a little sad leaving Iraq ... I like shoddy, drab old Baghdad, the mud walls and flimsy balconies, the narrow stinking lanes in the bazaars, the picturesque river front, and the great muddy river itself floating garbage to the sea. I like the men in their sweeping abbas who take life with a leisurely dignity, and the women who get on with it as drawers of water and hewers of wood—and on these infrequent wet days smacking their feet about in the cold wet mud ... I shall miss sand and palm trees, turtles, terrapins and watersnakes, lizards and geckos ... It will seem strange to call a person by the name of Ping Pong or Faithful

BAWDEN, Edward,
*Padre's Tent at Mersa
Matruh*, Watercolour,
$9\frac{1}{2} \times 23\frac{1}{4}$ins

Duck, instead of a homely Mohammed, Ali, Ahmed or Hussain; and stranger still to give up trying to practise stomachic gutterals or elusive vowel sounds for a manner of speech more resembling the tinkling of glass shaken in the wind.

Although the visit to China fell through there were compensations: a two-month trip accompanying an army expedition to the Jedda region, where it was hoped to kill off locust swarms at source; a second journey with Richard Wyndham to the Marsh Arabs in the Muntafiq; a week on the Tigris in a paddle steamer.

From each of these excursions Bawden sent back drawings. They sound pleasure trips, far from the sound of gunfire. But, as Bawden wrote, 'Arabia has no rivers; or roads. To progress by any means other than on foot is by knocking around on a slow bone-shaking camel or donkey.'

In July 1944, Bawden paid a brief visit to Tehran to depict 'Aid to Russia': transport, transit camps, supplies. In August he was recalled to England. Questions were being asked about the military relevance of some of Bawden's watercolours and it was felt that, since the centre of action had shifted to Europe, he should be on hand.

A visit to partisan-held Yugoslavia was considered. In the meantime a commission to paint Southampton docks led to an unusually open admission of failure. On October 12 Bawden wrote from Southampton,

> I have decided to return to London tomorrow. It shows a want of spirit on my part to give up the subject without having made any appreciable effort to tackle it, but the truth is I have felt no enthusiasm for boats which come in one day and are gone the next, or for cranes or other kinds of over-sized and restless machinery, even for the pathetic sight of wounded men being brought ashore on stretchers. I know very well that there must be ways of painting these fugitive scenes and many painters who would find it not unreasonably difficult to choose certain aspects; but for me the confusion, large scale and rapid movement cause a feeling of distress, anyway the important thing is lacking — that something which ought to touch the imagination. This is a sad confession, but I believe that it is better to admit defeat than to stay here any longer teasing my conscience.

By December Bawden was back in Rome, ostensibly en route for Yugoslavia. Coldstream was there 'holding his right arm over his chest like a bird with a broken wing', still ill with an abscess. But permits for Yugoslavia were not easy to get and Bawden, held in low esteem by the Public Relations Colonel in charge, was at the bottom of a long list of war correspondents. In February he was writing,

> For nearly a month I have worked in an unheated room in Ravenna ... My first plan was to get near to the front line. For one day and night I stayed at a Brigade H.Q. within about four miles of the firing; I went round a forward area and saw rather less than what might be seen in a

quiet country lane in England during summer manoeuvres. There was nothing of any pictorial interest, except three inches of snow … I came back to Ravenna in a jeep, my red raw ears flapping like rags for Communism, but so frozen I could not have sung the Internationale, even had I known the tune or the words. Ravenna is quite near enough to action, the thunder of gunfire is pretty continuous and on clear frosty nights the scream of shells can be heard faintly.

From Rome Bawden sent back seven drawings and an explanation,

All the drawings you will receive have been done with cold fingers. Sometimes, as I may have told you, I pee'd into my enamelled mug and then cupped my hands around it to try and receive back some of the heat I had lost. To work under uncomfortably cold conditions does not, I fear, confer any merit on the work itself, nor excuse any deficiencies; though if the former could be claimed then Thomas Hennell deserves the pot, as he tells me that on one occasion he painted an especially lovely sky in Iceland with his own water. I did not do that—when mine was cold I threw it from the front door into the street in true Latin style.

In March Bawden spent three weeks in Greece doing drawings of villages destroyed by the retreating Germans. On his return he wrote to the Committee: 'I hope there will be no excuse for a further renewal of my commission in June. The war is going so well that I look forward to seeing the ugly business finished before the summer. I confess that I am getting very tired of travelling and the waste of time it entails: I do want to get home and get some work done—work, too, of a peacetime character.'

In June he wrote them his last letter from abroad, quoting from an unposted letter of May 22.

I am at Udine, in sight of the snow on the Alps and at no great distance from the Austrian frontier which I am hoping to cross in two days time. The trek home of the so-called 'slave workers' is in evidence as this town is one of the collection centres. 18,000 came crowding in last night and this morning … It is a terrible sight—their physical condition is bad, but worse seeing the dull faces devoid of any expression of thought or emotion. Italian mostly, but there are Greeks, Czechs, and Yugoslavs: I spoke to two English girls, tarts I should guess, … also to some Latvian boys who had served in the German Army … Red Cross officers and priests were feeding the throng and packing them into transport supplied by the Army. I've been working for a couple of days on the subject … I did go on into Austria. Coldstream, who was with me in Udine for a day, went into Austria in advance, and returned two days later by road when I flew up by air … neither of us cared for the country or the people, or the rabble of Germans, Hungarians, and white Cossacks who were milling around.

The fortnight gained by this postponement [of his and Coldstream's return to England] is being spent by both of us in Florence—painting

BAWDEN, Edward,
*Zeminchel Tesfai*, Chalk,
ink and watercolour,
$19\frac{3}{4} \times 13\frac{3}{8}$ ins

the Ponte Vecchio and the Bailey bridge (a very graceful one) which replaces the beautiful S. Trinita ... In fact I am not very interested in the silly little hen houses that jut out over the river but what is very fine are the demolitions on each bank and at either end of the bridge.

One last word. It is difficult for me to express my gratitude for the generous support given me over the past 5 years ... If I may ignore the result of my own limitations as a draughtsman I would like to say that I have not been insensitive to the experience which came my way and allowed me to widen my own knowledge of the world and of my fellow-beings.

> Just as the lives of lions now are made
> Shabby with rifles,
> This great geography shrinks into sad
> And personal trifles.
>
> Roy Fuller, *In Africa*

On July 27, 1945, home at last, Bawden wrote, 'I landed at Liverpool on

Monday—an auspicious occasion as a taxi-man told me it was the first fine day for a month: I would not doubt his word as it has been raining ever since.'

Bawden, except for his experiences at Dunkirk and the torpedoing of the ship in which he was taking passage home, worked in war-zones rather than in battle areas. His paintings therefore tend to suggest the topography of war rather than its drama. More than any of his colleagues he seems to have had a free hand to hunt out the exotic sites of minor skirmishes. He was often ill, but in general he was right to feel himself privileged to see so much of the Middle East and southern Europe. The work he did, however, if often only marginally military, helped to fill out with richly evocative detail bare names on maps. His responsiveness to place makes his water-colours of the Sudan, Eritrea and the marsh areas of Iraq among his most engaging works.

Bawden was one of those painters for whom the war was an extension to his work—in terms of travel and experience especially—rather than an interruption. At the time he was appointed a war artist he was known mainly as a designer and illustrator. As a student at the Royal College his special subjects had been writing and illuminating. When he returned there to teach it was design and book-illustration.

During the 1930s Bawden supplemented his income by designing posters and wallpaper, as well as doing illustrations for books. He had moved to Great Bardfield in Essex, not far from Braintree, where he had been born. Until he was sent abroad to France in 1940 he scarcely left Essex and all the painting that he had done related to it.

It was not therefore predictable that so essentially provincial, in the true

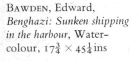

BAWDEN, Edward, *Benghazi: Sunken shipping in the harbour*, Water-colour, $17\frac{3}{4} \times 45\frac{1}{4}$ ins

sense, a character would adapt as well as Bawden did. But the self-reliance and independence, masked by reserve, that enabled him to find all he needed as material for his art where he happened to live, enabled him also to extract from wherever he went similar sustenance.

Bawden's war pictures are less concerned with directly military subjects than most. As a painter pre-war he had been drawn to landscapes, churches, odd juxtapositions of agricultural machinery, cattle markets and plants. His painting had tended to be schematised and angular, recognisably — despite its originality of colour — the marginalia of a designer.

The war opened his work out, giving him a new range of visual experience. He began to experiment with new techniques in the use of washes, using non-absorbent papers, so that although his methods are essentially studied, rather than instinctive, his war-time watercolours have a feeling of spontaneity and freshness.

Nevertheless, the lack of emotional involvement in all Bawden's work suggests certain real limitations, limitations that are the result of character rather than technique. The missing dimension is an imaginative one. Bawden the man rarely comes between the painter and the subject, and probably he would have regarded it as improper for him to have done so. His taste and wry vision affects his work, determining its standpoint, but his personality never transforms it.

The same, to a lesser extent, could probably be said of Edward Lear, a painter much admired by Bawden. But if there are losses in Bawden's fastidious, craftsmanlike approach there are also gains. The oddities of architecture and landscape are brilliantly transferred in such paintings as *The Emperor Menelik's Palace*, Addis Ababa, and *A Burnt Tukl at Gubba*, the

BAWDEN, Edward,
*The Emperor Menelik's Palace, the Old Gebbi,*
Chalk, ink and watercolour,
$18\frac{3}{4} \times 45\frac{3}{4}$ ins

Sudan, of the barrack buildings at Omdurman and of the harbour at Tobruk. The colours are both seductive and discreet.

In the Middle East Bawden developed in other ways: in a new-found ability to bring off rapid, atmospheric sketches of Baghdad bazaars and Saudi Arabian camel markets, of robed figures outside mosques or sheiks in their palaces.

He developed an entirely new line, swirling and congested, in contrast to the cool organisation of his landscapes and harbour scenes. He had begun in hospital at Colchester to do portraits of fellow patients, and in the Lebanon and Iraq, particularly, he produced a series of reflective studies of soldiers and camp followers. They have a warmth not found in his earlier work. Lastly, where Bawden's attachment to Essex had resulted in painting of purely local character, his travels in the Middle East brought to his watercolours a new lushness—palm trees, rivers, desert soil, brilliant light, old tombs, courtyards, fountains, mountain passes, marshes. Major battles were not being fought in these places, but armies had trained there and passed through. The scenes in Bawden's pictures were ones troops would recognise and remember.

# Anthony Gross

Testing North towards Tibet the cold
Austere horizon of coarse green pines
Holds trapped the waterfall. The wide sky throws
White clouds towards the annihilating snows.
                    Bernard Gutteridge, *Shillong*

If their handwriting is anything to go by Anthony Gross, whose career as a war artist crossed Bawden's at several points, could hardly have been more different as a character. Where Bawden's is large, sloping, and perfectly formed — page after page of diary and letter with scarcely an erasure — Gross's sprawls roundly in all directions. Where a page of Bawden offers the formality of an illuminated manuscript, Gross's diary has an artless spontaneity. Yet their age (Gross was two years younger), their training and their methods marked them as co-members of a generation. They shared more than an artistic climate.

Gross had been to Repton and the Slade. He lived at various times during the late 1920s and 1930s in France and he had married a French girl. He had studied engraving and etching, working at one period with Hayter. When war was declared Gross was collaborating on a cartoon film in Paris.

In February 1940 Gross wrote to Eric Kennington, whom he knew to be involved with the war artists' scheme. 'What I want to do now is to get to

GROSS, Anthony, *Coldstream, Irish and Welsh Guards in a Gymnasium*, Pen and wash, $7\frac{3}{4} \times 12\frac{3}{4}$ ins

GROSS, Anthony,
*Battery near Dover*,
Watercolour,
$14\frac{1}{2} \times 21\frac{5}{8}$ ins

France by some way or the other and paint in and behind the lines there.'
Gross pointed out his connections with France, his fluency in the language;
also that he had a car in Paris and contacts.

Kennington passed Gross on to Colin Coote at the War Office and
within a month Gross was reporting back to the Secretary of the War
Artists' Advisory Committee, 'I am down at Caterham and spent the day
at the Barracks. I went over the whole place, a veritable city, today.'

A week later Gross was writing to Sir Kenneth Clark, 'I feel that the
army has been much maligned over all these years, so much so that they
have been retiring into themselves and have developed a general knowledge of art and music and literature second to none. The other day I found
myself discussing Surrealism with two officers, one of whom rose in its
defence.'

From Caterham Gross moved to Shoeburyness, where he had the
congenial task of recording A.T.S. activities, and Catterick. In April he was
writing again to Clark, 'There is one thing I really enjoy in all this, and that
is being told to go somewhere, to do something I have never done before,
then the arriving there, finding myself face to face with the subject and at
last having to work out how to do it, starting from scratch. It is fascinating,
especially when I can remember periods where I seem to have gone on
sleeping for years doing more or less the same thing.'

Gross found barrack life agreeable and the officers hospitable. His
drawings reflect the orderliness of the routine and the conviviality of the
mess. A project to go to Norway had to be abandoned. Instead, in
December 1940, Gross found himself en route to Avonmouth to join the
troopship *Highland Monarch*.

On the long voyage out Gross produced numerous drawings of life on board ship, his convoy series. Their route took them out into the Atlantic, with subsequent stops at Freetown, Cape Town and Aden. Gross drew Freetown harbour and Table Mountain and made rapid, impressionistic studies of fencing lessons in the Red Sea and boxing matches in the Indian Ocean, of the ship's concerts and lifeboat drill, the desert at Suez. By nature a visual diarist, he was ideally suited to convey the particular flavour of shipboard life, with its contrived recreations, daily routines and exotic ports of call.

In one sense Gross was particularly fortunate. The *Highland Monarch*, because it had a cargo of seed potatoes, was directed to Egypt. The remainder of the convoy continued on its way to Singapore.

Gross found the British authorities in Cairo polite but not enthusiastic over his presence. Bawden was already there. On board ship Gross had made friends with a doctor posted to Alexandria and his first drawings, of hospitals, were made there.

The Italian pilots were giving everyone a hard time, and though Spitfires were just beginning to arrive, the mood at the various airbases Gross visited was faintly depressed. The company of Ardizzone, with whom he dined regularly at a Cypriot restaurant called *La Crystale*, did much to make these early weeks less gloomy.

GROSS, Anthony, *Battle of Egypt*, 1942, Pen and wash, $14\frac{1}{8} \times 21\frac{1}{2}$ ins

GROSS, Anthony,
*Camel Driver*,
Watercolour,
$14\frac{3}{4} \times 22\frac{1}{8}$ ins

Nevertheless, Gross got through a lot of work; as well as his hospital and airbase watercolours he made studies of Arab, Indian and Syrian troops. He went up to Palestine and Syria, en route for Persia where the 9th Army was being formed and to which Gross was to be attached.

On April 10, 1942, he was advising the Committee from Beirut, 'I have sent off another 17 drawings of Transjordan subjects mostly. Had a great time doing them in the Lawrence country. Meeting Bedouins and having beanfeasts with them in correct manner … About to start on new series before setting out for Persia via northern route if possible. Lebanon is very beautiful.'

These drawings, rolled up and sent home in empty shell cases, are some of Gross's most attractive: studies of desert patrols, camel regiments, Arab legionaries, Free French units. These nomad soldiers, roaming lonely and romantic country in their colourful costumes, were a pleasant contrast to the advance dressing stations, blood transfusions, ambulance trains and casualty depots that had been the main subjects of Gross's Western desert work.

In due course Gross was summoned back to Cairo for transfer to the Indian Army. The Battle of Alamein was in full swing, the fate of Stalingrad remained in the balance. Marauding cavalry at exercise in the uplands of Syria, however stimulating to paint, had begun to seem rather too peripheral for the continued lavishment of Gross's attentions.

By early January 1943, Gross was embarked on a troopship, having sent home a shopping list of watercolour paints: '20 tubes of viridian green, 15 tubes of yellow ochre, 12 Chinese white, 10 Vandyke brown,' etc.

They were seven or eight weeks at sea, stopping at Basra to pick up Polish refugees and deposit them in India. In Delhi Gross reported to Brigadier Jehu and was despatched to the Arakan, to record the building of the Imphal road.

In many ways Gross's year in the Middle East seems, in retrospect, merely to have been a period of rehearsal for his work in India. The Middle East had other war artists but Gross was the first to travel extensively with Indian and other local forces on their home soil. Much of Gross's desert drawing had been to do with Indian Army units, especially during the time of Alamein. Now he was to accompany them at the height of the Arakan campaign.

> Grey monkeys jibber, ignorant and wise.
> We are the ghosts, and they the denizens;
> We are like them anonymous, unknown,
> Avoiding what is human, near,
> Skirting the villages, the paddy fields
> Where boys sit timelessly to scare the crows
> On bamboo platforms raised above their lives.
> Alun Lewis, *The Jungle*

Gross's own diary gives a vivid picture of his time in eastern India. His journey down from Calcutta to Brigade Headquarters in the jungle was made by paddle-steamer, lorry and sampan. Mainly he travelled by river, as much out of sight of patrolling Japanese aircraft as currents would allow. Finally he arrived at a landing stage hidden in a mango swamp,

> We ran the sampan well under the bank … A mule was waiting for my kit. A battery opened up somewhere on my left. The track skirted paddy (rice) fields and finally entered a jungle of bamboo, mangoes and jack fruit. A sentry challenged me. I had arrived at Brigade H.Q. A guide took me by devious paths to visit the battalions. First I found the Lancashire Fusiliers sitting up on Pentlebury Hill overlooking the Temple of Rathedaung. Abandoned cattle were grazing peacefully on paddy fields in no-man's-land, while beyond, at what seemed a stone's throw, were the wooded hills of the Japs. In this thick scrub they were invisible, not a movement indicated the enemy. Occasionally a salvo of shells shook the air, then out of the vegetation on the other side little puffs of white smoke slowly rose. Later I visited the Rajputana Rifles, where I made a detailed drawing of the Jap position.

Gross was later to describe the extraordinary light of the Arakan, filtered through bamboo, as being 'like the light in paintings of the Italian Renaissance', every detail visible.

Soon Gross was exploring the terrain on his own, sometimes walking, sometimes riding.

> A tree with grapes of intense vermilion flowers, an over-grown cactus with little cups at the extremities of its fat twigs, were my landmarks. Birds of a brilliant yellow or blue flew around me … I remember finding a battery of Sikhs, who when they realized I was drawing them, phoned through to their commander for permission to stop firing to arrange themselves more decorously for the picture. Such a brushing of long hair, twirling of moustaches, combing of beards and winding of turbans, till, when they were all satisfied, they took up their positions by the gun again and gazed at me as fiercely as they could.

From the Arakan hills Gross went off by mule and ferry to paint pagodas, returning up the Mayu river to make drawings of advanced dressing stations and artillery observation posts. Here they came under regular fire from Japanese snipers embedded on the skyline above them. Whenever voices were raised in English they were answered by Japanese mortar fire.

Finding the area eventually 'too dicey for comfort', as he later recorded, Gross decided to make for Laungchaung where the Rajput Regiment was installed.

> A doctor and I set off on horseback over the Arakan Hills. Magnificent scenery as we slowly made our way up the pass, sometimes dismounting and walking up the beds of streams, the horse splashing in the shallow water while we leapt from stone to stone. Behind us the sea, till, coming over the crest, we looked down into the Mayu Valley, where the river winds with its many backwaters down to the sea at Akyab. That night, very saddle-sore, we encamped in a temple beside an enormous over-turned Buddha looking up into the sky.

Shortly afterwards Gross was accompanying units of the Indian Navy in an M.L. as they engaged the Japanese off Dombaik.

The 14th Army was being formed at Imphal, one of their immediate tasks being the building of a road into Burma. Gross left the Arakan, making his way to Chittagong and thence by train into Assam. Soon they were in the Naga Hills.

> Small groups of Naga tribesmen stood around in their picturesque costume … Later we gave them a lift and looking back into the interior of the truck, the Nagas, with their strange beads and ear-rings, their cloaks of matted grass and brilliant red, their intricate leggings of woven bamboo thread, their spears, looked like a cart-ful of chorus for an Italian opera. We passed many teams of these fierce head-hunting tribesmen engaged on building roads or perched high up above us hewing out the face of the cliff.

Eventually, climbing into mountain country, among pine forests covered in orchids, they arrived among the Chin Levies, fancifully attired tribes-men who had been holding off the Japanese for months with little more than knives and flint-locks. The Chin Levies' uniform, consisting of turbans, blankets and anything else they fancied, was recognisable by the distinguishing feather worn on their headgear.

As well as the Levies, whose job was to keep a constant eye on Japanese positions and patrols, the Chin Hills held Gurkha battalions and other tribesmen, such as the Animist Hakas, with their long hair and top-knots.

Gross immediately found himself at home in the Chin Hills, painting as many varieties of soldier as he could find. The Chins had their own artists for the recording of funerals and the painting of corpses. Gross developed a technique of adding water to Indian ink for greater fluency and to prevent drying out. His experience, he remarked on his return, had been one of 'enormous intensity'.

The journey back to the new road involved a march of nearly five hundred miles. 'For days we marched along, high up the valleys 6,000 feet below us, treading softly on a carpet of pine needles, stopping at times to gather wild raspberries, to drink at a mountain stream.'

Gross now applied to join the 4th Indian Division which had been fighting in the Western desert. The campaign was virtually over, with the Allied armies already landed in Sicily, but Gross was able to paint the British and Indian troops—the Royal Sussex, Pathans, Sikhs, Dogras among others—comprising the division.

GROSS, Anthony, *Battle of Arakan*, 1943, Pen and wash, $14\frac{1}{8} \times 20\frac{1}{4}$ ins

The winter of 1943–4 Gross spent mainly in East Anglia, drawing troops preparing for the Second Front. It was intensely cold, and Gross, after his years in Egypt, Syria, India and Burma, felt it acutely.

Gross landed at 2 p.m. on D–Day at Arromanches, having sailed in a vast convoy, before transferring to a smaller landing craft. He jumped overboard into shallow water with soldiers of the R.A.S.C., holding his equipment over his head. On the journey across in the convoy he made numerous pencil sketches. On July 24 he sent one of his few reports back to the Committee.

> I am sitting in a wood and it is a very pleasant evening. As you will have heard I had a fairly peaceful landing even though it was distinctly wet. The whole thing was quite astonishing, though, and fantastic. Quite a feeling of unbelief as I trod the sands of France again and the first evening in a grand Normandy farm with walls built in grey like a castle and of similar dimensions. We knocked back glasses of cider and calvados 'à la Victoire' and rolled over sound asleep after the excitement and the unbelievable exertions of carrying a full pack and painting materials.

Gross, who by using his wits generally acquired for himself almost total freedom of movement, decided to make for Brittany where Resistance groups were at work 'cleaning up' the Vichy *militaires* and collaborators. He went into Paris by jeep in the wake of de Gaulle.

For most of the rest of the war Gross, conscious of the usefulness of access to transport, remained with the R.A.S.C. In Belgium he had brief meetings with Hennell and Richards. When the Allied armies crossed into Germany Gross found himself involved in the Rundstedt counter-offensive. He travelled up and down the Rhine making drawings, meeting up with the Russians in an accordion factory on the Elbe.

In March 1945 Gross had written to Sir Kenneth Clark about the desire of *La Jeune Gravure* to put on a show of Gross's war drawings.

> It seems to me an opportune time to hold such an exhibition in Paris, including only the best people. Muirhead and Stephen Bone, Henry Moore and Sutherland, Bawden, Ardizzone, Piper, Ravilious etc. ... Anglophil feelings are absolutely enormous in France today. The French painters are talking of nothing but war artists at the present moment as the first batch have just been appointed on lines inspired by our committee (they include Picasso ...)

Gross's list of 'the best' is fairly uncritical; it is hard to see, too, quite what French war artists could expect to achieve at that time with the war already in its final phase. At the time of Gross's letter the British, Canadians and Americans had all crossed the Rhine and the Russians were on the outskirts of Vienna.

In one of Gross's few other surviving letters to the Committee, written in January 1945, he put in a request for a paraffin stove to take to France. 'It is essential for my work as in rainy and cold weather my watercolours will not dry on the paper.'

For the most part Gross took care of himself on his travels. He was aware that if he wanted to go and paint those things that, as an artist, stimulated him, he would have to use ingenuity and cunning. He took the greatest possible advantage of the ambiguity of his situation. In this, as in all other matters, he was thoroughly professional.

Gross remarked, in a post-war interview, that he simply recorded what he saw. He could not discover any philosophy that would be applicable to his art.

It is an art without pretension. Gross worked on the spot, rarely from notes or memory. His drawings, as a result, have immediacy and tension. Their value as documentation is considerable: the faces and apparel of troops, whether British, Syrian or Indian, are as he drew them. His landscapes, with their scratchy, rapid strokes, their soft washes, have often the economy and elegance of Lear's.

Gross's war paintings are fluent, observant, comradely; he would be the last, one imagines, to claim that they make any profound comment on war, or on the nature of suffering.

GROSS, Anthony, *The Arrival at Lofoten*, 1941, Pen and wash, $21\frac{1}{4} \times 30\frac{3}{8}$ ins

# *William Coldstream*

> The soldiers camped
> In the rock-strewn wadi merge
> Like lizard or jerboa in the brown
> And neutral ambient: stripped at gunsite,
> Or splashing like glad beasts at sundown in
> The brackish pool, their smooth
> And lion-coloured bodies seem
> The indigenous fauna of an unexplored
> Unspoiled country: harmless, easy to trap,
> And tender-fleshed — a hunter's prize.
>
> Jocelyn Brooke, *Landscape near Tobruk*

William Coldstream's methods as a painter — austere, immensely pains-taking, deliberate — would not immediately have suggested him as a likely candidate for a war artist. Before the war he had, when not working in documentary film as a means of earning a living, painted mainly portraits, still-lifes, and nudes. He painted, among others, W.H. Auden, Christopher Isherwood and Stephen Spender, and, between 1934 and 1937, worked under John Grierson and Cavalcanti with the G.P.O. Film Unit.

Coldstream was an extremely slow worker, dedicated to the task of accurate representation. 'I find I lose interest unless I let myself be ruled by what I see,' Coldstream wrote in 1937 in an article in the *Listener*. In the Introduction to the catalogue of a 1962 travelling exhibition of Cold-stream's work, arranged by the Arts Council, Lawrence Gowing described how Coldstream tackled the issue:

> His task was not even to describe the subject, in any direct sense; de-scription, the application of a vocabulary, is in itself a kind of interference. He painted as if he needed only to *receive* the complex information. He needed a system by which it could be registered as if registering itself. The style which Coldstream began evolving in 1937, and which he has been steadily pursuing ever since, consists of a medium for scanning and registering, rather as the travelling electronic dot scans and registers ... The visual distinctions that comprise the experience are real things and the distances between them are real and measurable ... The impersonality of Coldstream's method is deceptive. The detachment is essential; it permits him to isolate for exact inspection the relationship, the engagement, the *interest* which is most precious to him ... The impersonal method and the disguise of a passively recording instrument are in fact the means of a most positive and decisive pictorial action. It cuts straight through a knot that now seems to bind a painter; it solves the contradiction between two kinds of belief, the old kind and the new, in the basic reality of art.

In 1938 Coldstream had opened, with Victor Pasmore and Claude Rogers, a School of Drawing and Painting at 12 Fitzroy Street. It moved later to the Euston Road, from which address the kind of painting done there took its name. In 1940, at the age of 32, Coldstream joined the Royal Artillery as a private soldier, being attached initially to the 5th Field Training Regiment at Dover. He has described, in an interview for the Imperial War Museum taped series *Artists in an Age of Conflict*, how from Fort Burgoyne he could see gunflashes on the French coast and during the Battle of Britain was afforded a grandstand view of the action.

He was not happy as a gunner. But, after a brief spell near Loch Lomond, he found himself transferred to Farnham and commissioned as a Camouflage officer, with the task of advising anti-aircraft units at Bristol and Bushey on the arts of concealment.

In 1943 Coldstream was appointed a war artist and on July 16 sailed in a Dutch troopship from Liverpool. While waiting for a ship he had begun work at Trent Park on a portrait of General von Thoma, who had been captured in the desert and was now in a P.O.W. camp. Coldstream was unable to finish it.

In the Clyde they joined a convoy, slowly making its way to North Africa. Coldstream disembarked at Algiers, and after some days in a transit camp on Algiers racecourse continued by cattle truck along the Tunisian coast to Sfax. From Sfax he went by ship to Alexandria.

In Cairo, where Coldstream reported to Colonel Astley, head of public relations in the area, conditions were almost back to normal. The desert fighting was over, the invasion of Sicily had been followed by the Allied capture of Naples.

COLDSTREAM, William, *The Bailey Bridge built by Royal Engineers over the Volturno river, Italy*, Oil, $11\frac{7}{8} \times 24\frac{1}{8}$ ins

Coldstream was housed in a tent, on a marvellous site four miles from the Pyramids, within sight of the 'green chessboard' of the Nile delta, its sailing boats and feluccas.

It was suggested that he attach himself to the Indian units stationed in Cairo and for the next few months Coldstream painted portraits of Sikhs, Gurkhas and Rajputs, whoever wanted to sit for him. The resulting portraits— *Havildar Ajmer Singh, Subedar Jaggat Singh, Havildar Thapa*— are among the most impressive of any painted during the war. Lawrence Gowing has written of them, 'The system that maps the visual evidence, like a shuttle passing to and fro to weave the ultimately credible fabric, begins to leave at each passage a mark, like a vivid stitch of the very thread that draws the form together. The marks record something very definite— not what is seen, but the tension, the "rightness", that puts what is seen in its place.'

In these studies of warriors between battles Coldstream gives to his Indian soldiers a nobility of bearing that is all the more effective for being unobtrusive. Their faces, dominated by the steadfastness of their gaze, look out at an uncertain future. There is no aggression in either their posture or their expression. But they look, unmistakably, men of valour, comfortable of deportment but finely strung.

There are only a few such portraits, for each took Coldstream many sittings, and there were to be no more until the very end of the war, when Coldstream did studies of a Jamaican airman and an Italian Prisoner of War.

In early 1944, however, Coldstream set off for Italy. He was based, initially, at Capua, on the Volturno river, just north of Naples. The front was some twenty miles off and Coldstream has described the curious situation in which troops would be taking part in the battles of Anzio and Cassino one evening and going to the San Carlo Opera in Naples the next.

In Capua Coldstream finished three pictures in marked contrast to the portraits done in Cairo: Capua Cathedral, the Bailey Bridge over the Volturno, and a Casualty Reception Station. All three are meticulously painted, in the familiar plotted and rectangular manner. They have no great relevance to war and Coldstream has admitted that it was the architecture that interested him, not the military implications of the subject.

From Capua Coldstream went up to Pisa and then across to Rimini. Both cities had been badly bombed. In Rimini Coldstream did numerous drawings of the ruins of the Tempio Malatestiano and a painting of the bombed Opera House. He began but failed to finish a painting of Florence.

When the war ended Coldstream was in Klagenfurt, a centre for concentration camp refugees. He sailed for home from Naples shortly afterwards.

It could scarcely be said that the war, though extending his range of experience, created any new dimensions in Coldstream as an artist. He worked on his portraits much as he would have done anyway, in his own

time, unhurriedly. The subjects merely were different.

Coldstream's approach to the job of being a war artist was diffident in the extreme. He had no illusions about his illustrative gifts, his temperamental or technical suitability for dealing with military subjects. Indeed, he seems to have felt remarkably little obligation to engage himself in them during his two years' service overseas. He was about as far removed, in his lack of facility, from Gross, Ardizzone and Bawden as it was possible to be.

Coldstream has remarked that he felt it was as much out of kindness as anything that he was employed as a war artist at all. His discreet affability of manner led him to be thought on occasions a secret agent. In a way he was one, on behalf of his own integrity as a painter and the obsessiveness of his vision. A dozen pictures is not much to show for so much travelling around and looking at things. But it is typical of Coldstream that there was no fudging of feeling, no short-cuts to production. What he could not feel about he did not paint.

COLDSTREAM, William,
*Capua Casualty Station,*
Oil, $35\frac{3}{4} \times 28\frac{1}{4}$ ins

# X
# CREWS AND CARRIERS

*Barnett Freedman, Leonard Rosoman,*
*John Worsley*

Oh *Cooks to the Galley* is sounded off
And the lads are down in the mess
But I lie down by the forward gun
With a bullet in my breast.

Charles Causley, *Song of the Dying Gunner*

## Barnett Freedman

It would scarcely have been possible to get off to a worse start as a war artist than Barnett Freedman did. His complaints, demands, and general assumption of airs resulted in Colin Coote, within a few weeks of Freedman's appointment as a War Office artist, writing to Dickey, Secretary of the War Artists' Advisory Committee, 'Personally, I can see no alternative to dismissing so cantankerous a fellow ... It really is more important to keep out the Germans than to take in Mr. Barnett Freedman.'

In due course matters were resolved and by the end of the war Freedman had produced a number of memorable paintings, most especially his group portraits: soldiers manning a Sheerness battery, the ship's company of H.M.S. *Repulse*, the crew of the submarine *Tribune*.

Before the war Freedman was known mainly for his posters, book jackets and the coloured lithographs he had made in 1929 for Siegfried Sassoon's *Memoirs of an Infantry Officer*. The son of Russian Jews who had settled in the East End of London, he had spent much of his childhood in hospital. The family were badly off but Freedman's precocious talent managed to get him grants to go, first, to St Martin's School of Art, and then to the Royal College.

He was 38 when war broke out. Invited to produce a series of drawings of the B.E.F. in France he was soon reporting from there, 'I think it was a mistake not to give us honorary [commissioned] rank.' On May 28 he posted back a progress report on his difficulties.

Arrived Calais, April 10, 1940. No person there had any knowledge of my coming and I hadn't the faintest idea where to go. I was told in

London that I would be taken to G.H.Q. but nobody knew where that was, of course.

I should have been in much better position to produce work if I could have had the following privileges:

(1)   for personal use, a car and driver
(2)   Special War Artists' licence
(3)   Field Rank: officer's uniform and no badges raised suspicion. I was terrified of being shot as a fifth columnist.
(4)   Compensation if killed.

Freedman was soon proposing that war artists should be absorbed into Intelligence and removed from the Press category, a suggestion that made

FREEDMAN, Barnett, detail from *Portraits of the Crew of* Tribune, Oil, 104 × 42ins

little headway.

Back in England Freedman, unable to get back to France and barred from restricted areas at home, expressed his dissatisfaction in a letter to Dickey:

> I am sick of the whole thing, and if anyone could get me a commission in the Army so that I might do a decent job of work (and there are a good many jobs I could do) I would willingly, bloodywell take it.

It was this letter, on top of endless complaints from him about the quality of the reproductions of his work, that so incensed Coote.

Miraculously, matters improved in the autumn. A task was found for Freedman which resulted in his being installed at the Grain Fort, Rochester, to produce paintings of the camouflaged guns and the crews manning them. 'I have nearly finished here', he wrote on October 20, 'a complete gallery of the officers who run the big guns.' These were 9·2s, belonging to the Grain Fort and Fletcher Battery, Sheerness. In the same letter Freedman observed, 'I am most anxious at some future date to do a complete cross-section on a major battleship — from the stoker to the Captain — the inside life of such a ship.'

In March Freedman's employment was terminated. Sir Kenneth Clark wrote to him with suggestions for poster work and a possible job for the Admiralty.

Both materialised. By July Freedman, commissioned to do a painting of a battleship gun turret, was writing home from H.M.S. *Repulse*, saying how pleased he was with everything. 'It is an exceedingly complicated affair and I will take about 4 weeks to make my working drawings.

'All the arrangements for my journey from the moment I left London

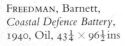

FREEDMAN, Barnett,
*Coastal Defence Battery*,
1940, Oil, 43¼ × 96½ ins

FREEDMAN, Barnett, *The Gun*, Oil, $23\frac{1}{4} \times 36$ ins

until I was piped aboard having been brought in the Captain's launch were perfect ... I should like to be here for years.'

Plainly, naval courtesy and efficiency suited Freedman a great deal better than the lack of interest shown by an army in retreat.

The *Repulse* portraits were an outstanding success, followed in 1943 by similar undertakings, the crew of the submarine *Tribune* and the personnel of an aircraft factory.

A commission followed for a painting of a W.R.N.S. Cypher office at the Naval Commander-in-Chief's Headquarters. A month after the Normandy invasion had begun Freedman was writing c/o Naval Party 1500, in France.

I have a typical 'Henri Merger' garret in a house that overlooks a vast activity. Thousands of men, and craft and engines of war almost cover the earth and sea and even the sky presents no restfulness. I have been labouring on a vast drawing (5 feet) in which I hope to get some record of this scene ... The drawing is on a panel ripped out of this shelled house and so if I get capsized on my way home in a week's time or so, I might float awhile on my own drawing ... I have been near the German lines once or twice which frightened me ... One cannot buy anything in the towns but I will bring you a camembert cheese if I can. I think of Cotman when I see the great barns and churches.

Freedman's stay in France was cut short by illness. Within weeks of his arrival he was back in England, incarcerated in the Gateacre Grange

Nursing Home, Liverpool. 'Without warning my tummy contorted itself to such a degree that I had to be rushed away and cut open ... I'm fed up to the teeth to think that I must be stuck here, with no work to do, and so much going on in France.'

By the autumn Freedman, though better, was still in hospital. His period in France had not, however, been wasted. He was able to work on and finish the large painting *The Landing in Normandy*, subtitled 'Arromanches, D–Day plus 20', as well as paintings of a Mulberry Harbour and a Headquarters Room watercolour.

Once he was able to accept the restrictions and circumstances under which he had to work Freedman proved a convivial companion, much liked by the officers and men whom he sailed with and painted. Having begun by painting aerodromes under construction in France during 1940 and portraits of sappers he ended up by becoming essentially a naval miniaturist. He continued to paint on a large scale from time to time—his *Coastal Defence Battery*, for example—but what he did best were the series of emblematic studies, private ikons in their way, of serving sailors. These are realistic, not romanticised in the Kennington manner; but in spite of, perhaps because of, their crudeness of feature they are curiously touching. Freedman's obvious affection and feeling for naval life, its particular kind of integration, enabled him to suggest the totality of the experience. Anyone who served at sea would recognise the authenticity of Freedman's portraiture, his ability to convey the particularly stylised and stilted nature of warship existence. His work, in its suggestibility, was the closest equivalent to the coloured postcards sent home by sailors during the First World War. The faces often seem to foresee their own destruction, their gaze already that of dead men.

FREEDMAN, Barnett,
*15 inch Gun Turret,*
*H.M.S.* Repulse, 1942,
Oil, 79 × 115 ins

# Leonard Rosoman

> The fires are grey; no star, no sign
> Winks from the breathing darkness of the carrier
> Where the pilot circles for his wingman; where,
> Gliding above the cities' shells, a stubborn eye
> Among the embers of the nations, achingly
> Tracing the circles of that worn, unchanging NO—
> The lives' long war, last war—the pilot sleeps.
>
> Randall Jarrell, *The Dead Wingman*

In 1939 Leonard Rosoman spent a month in late summer based in Honfleur, one of the prettiest fishing ports on the Normandy coast. It was the first real painting holiday he had ever had and it resulted in about twenty oils and gouaches, somewhat in the romantic manner associated with Sutherland. He was 25 and had come not long before from Durham University to take up a teaching post at Reimann's Art School.

Within weeks of his return from Honfleur war had broken out. Rosoman enrolled in the National Fire Service, operating from Maresfield Gardens in London, not far from where he lived. William Sansom and Stephen Spender were already attached to fire-stations in the area. After some months of desultory activity, when firemen were encouraged to lecture on and practise their peace-time pursuits, the Blitz began and Rosoman was involved in fighting fires all over London, most especially the docks and the City. He did numerous paintings of this time, including *Falling Wall*, a much-reproduced picture of a burning wall about to collapse and kill two firemen.

None of the paintings he did of the Blitz seemed to Rosoman successful on his own terms: too melodramatic, possibly, not subtle or distanced enough in approach. It is easy to see now how far their direct confronting of situations is removed from the fastidious obliqueness of Rosoman's later manner and why this should be cause for personal distaste. Nevertheless, these fire-fighting months produced subjects, made him aware of himself as a more graphic artist than he had imagined, and forced him to acknowledge relationships between men and machines he had scarcely envisaged. This relationship, the effect of machines on men, rather than men in control of machines, became the theme of nearly all his best war paintings.

Sometime in 1942, when the raids on London had begun to vary in intensity, Rosoman was drafted from his fire-station duties to an office job. The Home Office had written asking if he would like to work on illustrations for *The Fire Service Manual*, a task involving the factual recording of every conceivable sort of activity, from the tying of reef knots to the climbing of ladders. In this capacity Rosoman travelled all over the country for nearly 18 months, visiting local fire-stations.

He was still involved in this when, out of the blue, he was summoned to the Admiralty and invited, on condition that he was willing to go immedi-

ROSOMAN, Leonard, *A Radar Predictor*, Oil, 16 × 20 ins

ately to the Pacific, to become an official war artist. He accepted, and was duly given an honorary commission, with the rank of Captain in the Royal Marines. His initial commission was for six months from April 1, 1945 and was intended as replacement for Thomas Hennell who had been transferred to the Air Ministry for service in the Far East.

Rosoman was soon on board a troopship sailing in convoy down the Clyde. After the usual Atlantic zig-zag they steamed through the Straits of Gibraltar, eastward across the Mediterranean, down the Suez Canal and Red Sea, and finally across the Indian Ocean to Sydney. On board Rosoman kept a journal, and did numerous sketches of troopship life.

In Sydney, after a few weeks on shore, Rosoman was attached to the aircraft carrier *Formidable*, then under the command of Admiral Vian. Not long after his joining her, *Formidable* set sail up the east coast of Australia, past the Admiralty islands, for Japanese waters.

After a frantic cable for money Rosoman wrote what seems to have been his only letter of any consequence to the Committee:

I'm with the British Pacific Fleet in the flagship carrier and we're off the coast of Japan ... whilst in Sydney I wandered about the Fleet and rather liked the look of aircraft-carriers so sailed away in *Formidable*. I've become interested in all sorts of strange devices like Radar indicators, pom-poms, and planes with wings that fold up like a moth's. I'm making masses of studies of these things which, coupled with the Kamikaze business, seems just my cup of tea. There are lots of snags, of course—there's no space in which to work. I have a cabin but it has artificial light and is so small I practically have to paint in bed. Then there's the heat, which is unbelievable—painting in oil becomes a considerable physical exertion and costs pints of sweat. I paint absolutely nude when I'm in the cabin and as I'm a very untidy painter I tend to look like an Early Briton in war-paint. I want to get on to something big now so I shall probably return to Sydney where I have been given a studio …

I expect you've heard I had rather a dreary trip out … the biggest blow of all was when I arrived in Sydney and the cursed baggage people lost my trunks with all my materials in them. I chased these things for 2 weeks all over Southern Australia and eventually found them in New-castle, 500 miles away … I'm pretty happy, really, when one considers that I'm in a completely new and rather terrifying world. I have my depressions but the work goes on alright … May I enquire tentatively what happens when my 6 months is up?

ROSOMAN, Leonard,
*A Man Crouching in a*
*Hatchway during Action*,
Gouache, $19\frac{1}{4} \times 11\frac{3}{4}$ ins

Gregory replied sympathetically, 'You will have received a signal saying your leave has been extended for another 3 months...It is very much hoped you will be able to do some scenes of the signing of negotiations between Japan, Britain and other nations, and also scenes of the army of occupation and of the capitulation.'

It was in this period with the Royal Navy in the Pacific that Rosoman painted the series of pictures on which his achievement as a war artist rests. *Formidable* was frequently in action, but more to the point Rosoman was able to study and record at leisure the activities of the pilots and radar operators, the clumsy bumble-bee-like take-offs of Corsairs and Avengers that sometimes failed, the pin-point landings, the general insect-like stacking and manoeuvring of aircraft on the flight deck, the hive-busyness of the hangars. The self-contained world of a warship at sea, so alike in many ways to the workings of the natural world, the relationship of so many different constituent parts to the whole, became the real subject of his paintings.

It was less the ship as a weapon of aggression than the ship as a unit learning to live with itself, that Rosoman painted. He was particularly suited by nature to do this, since one of the basic themes of his paintings has always been the unpredictability of behaviour and events, the fragility and precariousness of human existence. Shipboard life, with its strange specialist tasks, its cocooned inhabitants, gave Rosoman in many ways an ideal subject, a stronger context, perhaps, for his elaborate, imaginative fantasies than any he subsequently discovered. While Rosoman was in *Formidable* a kamikaze pilot crashed into the flight deck, the whole ship briefly in danger. But he has said that he found the destructive aspect of warfare impossible to record; not for either technical or temperamental reasons but rather because he felt unable to deal with the experience satisfactorily within the context of his own painting. In the end, regardless of subject, a painter has to construct his own picture in his own way; it will only succeed as a work of art if the experience has been properly absorbed. Rosoman, perhaps inevitably as a war artist, always felt slightly apart from the other officers and men who had continual and specific functions related to the running of the ship. His pictures are, in that sense, detached; minutely observed, but not involved.

It was necessary for him to feel his way into a painting instinctively before he could do so aesthetically. A consequence may have been the limitation of his treatment, but the reward was that all his war pictures are recognisably his, in his own idiom. They give no impression of having been proposed.

Rosoman declined the offer to paint the Japanese surrender, suggesting he was unsuitable for such a commission. Instead he proposed that he fly to Hong Kong and paint the ships sunk in the harbour. Several richly evocative pictures of junks, in sumptuous reds and yellows, were the result.

Writing about this time much later in the *London Magazine* (August 1962) Rosoman observed:

ROSOMAN, Leonard,
*A Crater in the Naval
Dockyard, Hong Kong*, Oil,
$21\frac{1}{2} \times 29\frac{1}{2}$ ins

When I went to the Far East as a war artist and lived aboard an aircraft-carrier, I had time to see a war-life that I found stimulating. The odd and the unexpected are interesting and dangerous and I had always fallen for the quirks of life: what I wanted was to imbue them with a stable, permanent quality, to control the sense of horror which lay beneath the consciousness. I'm the worst portrait painter and I can only see people as puppets caught unawares. To watch a man sitting, trapped almost, in the flower-like interior of a radar predictor was beautiful. The aeroplane folds its wings and crouches on the flight deck. These things must be felt with the senses, not just used in terms of interesting shapes.

The glimpses of the landscape round Hong Kong were a revelation. Instead of the subtle tones and muted colours of Chinese painting, there were strident reds and chrome greens spattering the hills and the intense greenish black of the coolies' dress gave out a spooky smell. I'd never seen a Chinese junk before and I couldn't believe that they were boats floating on the brown water. They looked like floating grand pianos and I had thoughts of Salvador Dali.

The experience of big-ship organisation and contact with more exotic environments than he had known were important for Rosoman. In his best aircraft-carrier pictures he conveys a sense of privileged secrecy, the fluke of being able to observe, from a unique vantage point, extraordinary goings-on. This has always been an aspect of Rosoman's art: war-machines, in their fragile finery and unpredictable assignations, acted as substitutes for the bizarre human encounters he has eavesdropped on in all his later work.

Rosoman's aircraft are quite different from those painted by Paul Nash and Ravilious; more specific, more inhabited. At the same time they have a lyrical gleam and finish to them, so that, however lethal the subject matter, the effect is of transient butterfly beauty. Ravilious and Nash were confined to the north, Rosoman's ships sail Pacific waters or founder in the South China Sea. The atmosphere is almost one of liberation – not so much from confinement or oppression, as of climate. Winters of grinding European war, the Blitz and black-out, the absence of light, have been left behind; the last acts, in which these strange insect-like creatures swarm up protectively over their floating hives, are played out in sunlight.

Rosoman's naval pictures are intense because of their self-scrutiny. They are to do with war only in the sense that they deal with equipment related to war. Battle is the final act in a long process, intricately organised, that may never be realised. Meanwhile, in richly blue oceans, the communion between pilots and their planes, planes and ships, mechanics and sailors, officers and ratings, continues ceaselessly, whether there is resolution or not.

McGrath, Raymond,
*Wings*, 1940,
Watercolour, 15 × 22 ins

# John Worsley

> I see men as trees suffering
> or confound the detail and the horizon.
> Lay the coin on my tongue and I will sing
> of what the others never set eyes on.
> Keith Douglas, Desert Flowers

John Worsley was the only serving sailor to transfer from active service to the status of war artist. Albert Richards had, with unhappy results, made the change from paratrooper, and one or two other artists—Ardizzone, for example—had served briefly in the armed forces before taking up their peace-time profession on a war basis. The war provided Worsley—aged 20 when it broke out—with a subject as well as an occupation. If he thereafter never found a theme or style of the same importance, his work between 1940 and 1945 probably gets as close to conveying the quality of shipboard life—in his case Armed Merchant Cruisers and L.C.T.s (Landing Craft, Tank)—as anyone else's. Moreover, he was the only war artist to be taken prisoner and survive (Thomas Hennell was the only other to be captured) and his drawings, smuggled out of Marlag 'O', provide a detailed commentary on camp life.

Worsley's first involvement with the War Artists' Advisory Committee took place in May 1940, when a number of pencil sketches he submitted from the Armed Merchant Cruiser *Laurentic* were purchased. Worsley, the son of a naval officer, had spent some of his childhood in Africa before coming home to Brighton College and Goldsmith's School of Art. He had joined up in 1939, being taken on as a Midshipman and drafted to *Laurentic*, an ex-P and O liner fitted with 6″ guns. *Laurentic* spent most of 1940 on the northern patrol, between Iceland and Greenland, her task being the interception of German raiders. In this capacity she sank a German ship masquerading as Norwegian before herself being sunk off the coast of Ulster by a U-boat. Worsley was one of the survivors, picked up from a lifeboat by a destroyer. On his survivor's leave he painted a picture of the *Laurentic* sinking.

A month before *Laurentic* went down Worsley had written to the Committee complaining about his fee, 5 guineas for three drawings. 'On the spot sketches by artists taking an active part in this war are not so numerous and I feel that the Artists Advisory Committee might realize this more than they do.' Worsley was quite right, except in the assumption that such work might automatically be valuable. His grievance, however, puts into perspective the differing criteria by which war art can be judged, that is to say its authenticity as document or its quality as a work of art. The War Artists' Advisory Committee had, by and large, set its face against dramatic reconstructions of events unwitnessed by the artist, though an initial distaste for such pictures was subsequently modified. Nevertheless, Worsley was not alone in feeling that most war art was produced away

WORSLEY, John, *Smoke on the Horizon*, 1940, Wash, $9\frac{1}{2} \times 12\frac{7}{8}$ ins

from the real action; it was a common complaint among artists themselves that lack of facilities and bureaucratic obstruction senselessly confined them to marginal activities. Worsley was, in a sense, privileged: for he had the right to be where he was. However much he was handicapped by having to undertake the full duties of a watch-keeping officer he was able to use the time at his disposal in a far more intimate fashion than those artists who felt themselves welcomed only on sufferance. Worsley, himself, when he became an official war artist, immediately felt the difference.

Worsley returned from survivor's leave to do a course at King Alfred, Hove, emerging as a Sub-Lieutenant, R.N.V.R. and being appointed to H.M.S. *Lancaster*, an American-built destroyer and one of a class notorious for its rolling qualities in even the gentlest seas.

From *Lancaster* he returned to an Armed Merchant Cruiser, *Rampura*, finally joining the cruiser *Devonshire* on escort duty between Aden and Fremantle. Mostly they accompanied large liners converted into troopships for the purpose of ferrying Australian soldiers to and from the war in North Africa.

Worsley did a number of sketches during these voyages through the Indian ocean but it was only when *Devonshire* was paid off and he was appointed to the staff of C.-in-C., Mediterranean, as a war artist, that he was able to seek subjects of his own choosing.

On his appointment Worsley had been encouraged by Admiral Sir William James not to loaf about at Malta but to put his head 'into the lion's mouth'. This Worsley proceeded to do. He took part in the Sicily and Salerno landings, making drawings of the landing craft going in and out of the Mellili Caves in Sicily, used as storage for mines.

After a spell on the monitor ship *Roberts* Worsley returned briefly to Malta. From Malta he flew to Taranto, setting off from there up the

Adriatic coast to an island base south of Pola. The scheme was for motor torpedo-boats to ferry and land saboteurs, usually disguised as monks, their cassocks bulging with grenades, just south of Venice, at Chioggia. Here they would contact the British P.O.W.s now on the loose and make with them for Yugoslavia.

Several such sorties were successful, but eventually the small party of which Worsley was a member was sighted by a German seaplane and attacked. They took cover on an island but were rounded up by a German raiding party.

As far as naval activity was concerned this was the end of Worsley's career as a war artist. 'I felt', he said, discussing his invasion of Sicily drawings, 'because I was a war artist I was sort of like a referee. I was on the touchline watching and therefore nobody would hurt me.'

Worsley was sent, first, to Ljubljana, then to a P.O.W. camp, Marlag, outside Bremen. The Marlag camp had R.N.R. officers on one side—Marlag Nord—and naval officers on the other, Marlag 'O'. German officers occupied the space in between.

Since few sailors were captured—they usually drowned—Marlag was a comparatively small camp. Nevertheless, it housed three naval V.C.s—

WORSLEY, John, *Away Walrus*, 1943, Oil, 48 × 36 ins

WORSLEY, John,
*South-west Corner of Naval
Officers' Prison Camp in
Winter*, Watercolour,
$19\frac{1}{4} \times 25\frac{1}{2}$ ins

Beatty, Cameron, Place—and Worsley did portraits of them.

Worsley, aware that his capture had been partly due to his own reckless-ness, felt obliged to work as hard as materials and circumstances allowed. The record of his period at Marlag 'O'—from late November 1943 until liberated by the 11th Armoured Division—is therefore a very full one. The subjects range from negro seamen to loading wood, from the contents of a Red Cross parcel to filling in escape tunnels, from an illicit alcohol still to the shower-room.

Worsley was set free from Lübeck, the prisoners having been marched 80 miles at one stage and been fired on by British fighters, despite pushing a cart draped with a Union Jack. Several were killed.

In Lübeck Worsley met Anthony Gross, and after a few days enjoying the feel of freedom was flown home in a Lancaster. He brought most of his drawings out in containers made by sticking together Crim milk tins salvaged from Canadian Red Cross parcels.

Worsley had painted one or two large oils during the early part of the war, including *The Loss of the Laurentic*, the picture itself being lost through enemy action, so that it had to be repainted from a photograph of the original. He now painted several more, Naval and Marine P.O.W.s on the march between Bremen and Lübeck, a portrait of Admiral Sir John Cunningham, Commander-in-Chief, Mediterranean Fleet, and a portrait of Field Marshal Montgomery.

For the Cunningham portrait Worsley was flown out to Naples in December, 1945. He painted the Admiral at his naval headquarters in the Villa Emma, a place of Nelsonian attachment, with the Bay of Naples in the background. Worsley had great regard for the chain-smoking Cunningham and the portrait has a romantic ruggedness, unlike the faintly shifty look given to the features of Montgomery. The Montgomery is not, in fact, a good likeness; the Field Marshal's briskness was not much to Worsley's taste. Worsley painted him during several interrupted days in Germany, the one humanising touch he found—and painted—being the canaries in Montgomery's caravan. On remarking on these to a staff officer Worsley was disillusioned to be told that Montgomery only had them installed to test for gas.

In a fairly literal and professional way Worsley did a good job, both before and during his time as a war artist. His experiences, particularly in terms of the Navy, were unique. He was obliged to work from rapid sketches made on the spot, but some of these, like *Smoke on the Horizon*, where a group of officers leaning over the parapet looking through binoculars are drawn from the back of the bridge, are extraordinarily effective. His drawings, free from preconceived impositions of idiom, grow suggestively from their subjects. In such oils as the portrait of Admiral Sir John Cunningham Worsley fulfilled a commission with a no-nonsense directness that nevertheless pays colourful tribute to naval legend.

In a letter dated October 8, 1945, Worsley wrote in rather pained terms to the organisers about a show of war art at the National Gallery. 'I see that there are none of my P.O.W. watercolours there...I took so much trouble, and underwent such considerable hazard (including hiding much from the Germans) to get them out of Germany and in a small way justify my capture, that the disappointment was extreme. I even constructed a container from Red Cross milk tins, which I carried for an eighty-mile march, under strafing from fighter planes, to get them here.'

The omission was repaired.

*left,*
WORSLEY, John, *The Contents of a Red Cross Parcel,* Oil, 30 × 24 ins

*right,*
WORSLEY, John, *Admiral Sir John Cunningham, K.C.B., M.V.O., Commander-in-Chief, Mediterranean Fleet,* Oil, 35 × 28 ins

# XI

# SEAPLANES AND SPITFIRES

*R.V. Pitchforth, Frank Wootton*

> You shouldn't cry
> Or say a prayer or sigh.
> In the cold sea, in the dark.
> It isn't a lark
> But it isn't Original Sin—
> It's just a Beau going in.
>
> Gavin Ewart, *When a Beau Goes In*

## R.V. Pitchforth

R.V. Pitchforth was among the quickest-working, most versatile and prolific of all war artists. He was forty-four when the war began, having served 1915–18 with the Royal Garrison Artillery. Despite having been badly deafened during his first war service he was invited early on in 1940 to take on A.R.P. subjects. Pitchforth, born and brought up in Wakefield, had been a member of the London Group and showed regularly at the Royal Academy, of which he became an Associate in 1942. His fluent technique made it easy for him to turn his hand from bomb damage to A.R.P. practice, from the building of R.A.F. rescue launches to the construction of hangars, from seaplanes and submarines to parachute landings, from convoys to deep-sea divers.

After spending most of 1940–1 in London, Manchester and Birmingham on such comparatively humdrum subjects as the repair of telephone cables, factory routines and the testing of gun-barrels, Pitchforth moved on to the Air Ministry. His first job, on the furnace platform of a Sheffield steel works, he later described as being 'like fairyland ... the brilliant bright light when the furnace doors were opened, the steel workers with their sweat rags and blue glasses watching to see how it was cooking'. About the gun-barrel factory he commented that, instead of a lot of workers in an atmosphere of dirt, smoke and steam, it was more 'like the Science

Museum, with only a few workers around in clean white coats testing—
nothing to get at pictorially'.

PITCHFORTH, R.V.,
*A Parachute-Landing*, Oil,
$21\frac{3}{4} \times 49\frac{3}{4}$ ins

Later in Sheffield Pitchforth saw the gun turret of the battleship *King
George V* being assembled; 'one couldn't put a knife blade between the
joints'.

To save humping his painting equipment about Pitchforth got into the
habit of leaving it on bombed sites when he was painting them. Only in the
House of Commons did he ever lose anything; then it was his brushes and
paints but not his drawings.

Pitchforth's first subjects with the R.A.F. were speed-boats, but he was
soon off to Plymouth and Lee-on-Solent, enthusiastically accepting any
commission that was offered. His watercolours of night exercises, of
seaplanes landing and taking off, of parachutes opening, rise above the
conventional largely because of their sense of movement. Pitchforth's
handling of similar subjects is less stylised and proprietary than that of
Ravilious and Rosoman, but his delight in marine and aerial activity gives
his best pictures a genuine feeling of exhilaration.

In 1942 Pitchforth was at a maintenance unit at Henlow, where his
subjects ranged from test pilots to aerodrome layouts. From here he went
to Portland harbour and then on to a battle school in North Wales. In
October 1943 Pitchforth was taken on by the Admiralty, a transfer that at
last got him out of England. He painted motor gunboats in action, convoys
forming up in Londonderry, in Scottish waters and in the Mediterranean,
divers going down off Gibraltar. In 1944 Pitchforth was in Algiers, in 1945
in Colombo and Rangoon, in 1946, on his way home, in Durban and
Simonstown.

Pitchforth's work, encompassing the activities of all three Services, has
immediacy and dash. He never seems to have been held up in his response

PITCHFORTH, R.V.,
*Sunderland taking off at
Plymouth*, Watercolour,
$14\frac{1}{4} \times 20\frac{3}{4}$ ins

by preoccupations with painterly problems. His reactions to places and machines were instinctive and lively, and nearly all his pictures have not only dramatic content but lyrical finish. What is missing, however, is the human dimension: the tragic sense that questions and analyses.

All those subjects that Pitchforth handled so dexterously and proficiently, in so many parts of the world, were related, after all, to warfare;

PITCHFORTH, R.V.,
*Beauforts*, Watercolour,
$21\frac{1}{4} \times 29\frac{1}{2}$ ins

many of the men in his aircraft and gunboats, his battle schools and destroyers, would shortly be killed.

His elegant journalese suggests none of this, merely that we are witnessing displays of skill and organisation. Pitchforth was not alone among war artists in limiting himself to surface delineations, but the effect ultimately is of a kind of heartlessness, as unintentional as it is unconscious. That war has to do with death is not a truism that requires much spelling out but awareness of it is present in all the best writing and painting that came out of the war. Pitchforth's genial adaptability was probably the main obstacle that prevents his pictures from usually doing more than charm.

PITCHFORTH, R.V., *Gibraltar Night Defences*, 1944, Watercolour, $22\frac{1}{4} \times 30\frac{3}{4}$ ins

# Frank Wootton

They worked all night with cardboard and with wood
to make those dummy planes to hoodwink the foe,
and in the chilly morning solitude
wheeled out the dummies to places they should go
on the dispersal fields, and went away;
the hours passed uneventfully and even,
no reconnaissance planes were overhead that day.
They evacuated in the twilight, just after seven,
and when they'd gone the Germans flew above the drome
and by each plane they dropped a wooden bomb.

Herbert Corby, *Reprisal*

There was a period in 1942 when the Air Ministry, sceptical about the accuracy of Paul Nash's aeroplanes, tried to get him replaced by Frank Wootton. A technique that in terms of machinery was essentially impressionistic had led to progressive criticism. This would not be likely to apply to Wootton, a meticulous technical artist with a specialist interest in and knowledge of aircraft.

Wootton is an illustrative painter pure, if not simple, but nevertheless one whose representational skills and glossy colour make his work comparable to some neo-realist art of the late 1960s. It differs from the latter, mainly, in that where realist and superrealist art were unmitigatedly hard-edged, Wootton's backgrounds — empty skies, cloud formations, target areas, landscapes — were conventionally treated. He gave to weather the same serious scrutiny as meteorologists do.

It was always likely that such work would recommend itself more to service pilots than to art critics and teachers of fine art. It was largely as a result of the interest taken in his work by Air Commodore Peake, Director of Public Relations to the R.A.F., that Wootton was given the task in 1941 of doing technical drawings for Training Command, to be used for instructional purposes. From this simple beginning Wootton flew to Normandy in 1944 to record R.A.F. subjects during the last stages of the war in Europe; to India; and finally to Burma. From each of these theatres he sent back paintings of Lancasters, Beaufighters, Hampdens, Blenheims, B-25s, Mosquitoes, Boeings, Hurricanes, Typhoons and other aircraft, that were unlikely to lead to raised eyebrows in the officers' mess. In fact the strictest purist would not have faulted them, for Wootton took immense pains to get every detail right. The aircraft as hero was the subject of each one of his paintings, its crew and context subsidiary.

It is easy to dismiss such painstaking picture making, lacking as it is in any subtleties of tone or originality of composition. Wootton's aircraft are in reality coloured models sent soaring into flight against painted skies. Their slickness works against them in the sense that while everything looks photographically accurate there is a general feeling of unreality. Wootton flew in many of these aircraft and his various backgrounds—whether Burma, Normandy, or India—are painted at first-hand. His paintings of action—a Beaufighter attack on a channel convoy, Lancasters crossing the Alps, Typhoons demolishing German tanks with rockets at Falaise—suggest that this is what it looked like but not what it felt like. Everything has been cleaned up to reveal the identifying characteristics of individual aircraft.

Wootton was not without training, for he had left Eastbourne College of Art in 1932 with its Gold Medal and a travelling scholarship. He had painted advertisements for de Havilland and worked for the Ministry of Information.

In that he supplied what at least some of them wanted, the R.A.F. were lucky to have Wootton. No other painter could have brought the same technical interest—or proficiency, for that matter—to the re-creation of bombing raids and air battles. His pictures of Wellingtons taking off, lone Spitfires on reconnaissance, Flying Fortresses and Blenheims among the clouds, show genuine affection. If the pilots in Wootton's work are generally invisible, mere blobs at the controls, the loneliness of their situation is real. Similarly, his paintings of Hawker Harts, flying in formation over the Himalayas, with Nanga Parbat in the distance, or a B-25 Mitchell coming in low above the Shwe Dagon Pagoda, outside Rangoon, convey the true exhilaration and adventure of flying. The planes themselves may have been finished from models or studied on the ground, but what he painted Wootton had seen for himself.

There exist many striking photographs of air bombardments but Wootton was able to co-ordinate the various elements into dramatic canvases quite outside a photographer's range. His pictures, as of the annihilation of German tank columns at Falaise, were often begun before the smoke had cleared away. It was his limitation that whereas he could get all the details right he never quite managed to produce more than an illustration.

WOOTTON, Frank, *Rocket-firing Typhoons at the Falaise Gap, Normandy*, 1944, Oil, $41\frac{1}{2} \times 59\frac{1}{2}$ ins

# *Postscript*

Here with the desert so austere that only
Flags live, plant out your flags upon the wind,
Red tattered bannerets that mark a lonely
    Grave in the sand;

A crude oblong stone to hold some mortal
Remains against a jackal's rooting paws,
Painted with colour-wash to look like marble
    Through the heat-haze...

R.N. Currey, Burial Flags

Several of the more prolific war artists—whether employed on specific commissions or on a salaried basis—have found no mention in the text, although represented by illustrations. Taste is, after all, a personal matter and my reason for omitting consideration of such as Leslie Cole, William Dring and Stephen Bone—Cole worked mainly, and rather derivatively, in the neo-romantic idiom in Malta and the Far East, Dring on naval and R.A.F. portraits, Bone with the Navy—is simply that, despite their competence and facility, they make little distinctive contribution to war art. Although they have nothing in common with each other their treatment of widely differing subjects lacks presence in terms of either art or war.

Nevertheless, the vaults of the Imperial War Museum (and those of numerous other galleries and museums to which paintings acquired under the 1939–45 war artists' scheme were allocated) contain impressively individual pictures by artists who painted only occasional works on war subjects. Outstanding among these is Meredith Frampton's large dominating oil of Sir Ernest Gowers and other senior officers in the London Regional Civil Defence Control Room, an ultra-realist painting of 1943 that succeeds both as psychological portraiture and as a suggestive assemblage of detail. The busyness of a room where information is co-ordinated and acted upon has been briefly interrupted, but—as in a film freeze—the atmosphere of controlled tension and decision-making will be resumed the moment the painter leaves.

FRAMPTON, Meredith, *Sir Ernest Gowers, K.C.B., K.B.E., Lieutenant-Colonel A. J. Child, O.B.E., M.C., and K. A. L. Parker, in the London Regional Civil Defence Control Room*, Oil, $58\frac{1}{8} \times 66\frac{1}{4}$ ins

BONE, Stephen, *Up the Tower*, Oil, $29\frac{5}{8} \times 29\frac{5}{8}$ ins

Keith Henderson, 56 when war broke out and envisaged at one stage as more suitable for attachment to the R.A.F. than Paul Nash, produced a mere handful of oils, but his studies of air-crew and aerodromes have genuine power. Laura Knight's *Take Off*, a huge oil showing the interior of a bomber has similar tension and immediacy. Henry Carr, who had served in France 1915–18 with the Royal Field Artillery, mainly concentrated on portraits of V.I.P.s — Generals, the Bey of Tunis, V.C.s — but his *Vesuvius in Eruption*, (1944) and *Parachute Drop* (1943) are pictures that vividly evoke specific phases of the war. Raymond McGrath's meticulous 1940 water-colours of hangars and the assembling of bombers have the purity and accuracy of architectural drawings, at the same time conveying a lyrical feeling for the beauty of aircraft. Norman Wilkinson, one of the pioneers of naval camouflage and a war artist in 1914–18, painted effective anec-dotal pictures of naval incidents, later moving on to R.A.F. constructional subjects.

Edward Burra's *Soldiers at Rye*, a large watercolour painted in 1942 and now in the Tate Gallery, introduced elements from different periods of history — Mexican, Spanish — into an allegorical painting similar in tone to Wyndham Lewis's earlier *The Surrender of Barcelona*. Half-a-dozen round-buttocked and tin-hatted soldiers dominate the foreground, their grimac-ing scarlet-beaked masks and louche air of fancy-dress confusion suggestive of chaos. Burra, who was in Madrid when the Spanish Civil War broke out, has made his home town of Rye, in 1942 full of Canadian soldiers, a

BURRA, Edward, *Soldiers at Rye*, 1942, Gouache and watercolour, $40\frac{1}{4} \times 81\frac{1}{2}$ ins

EVANS, Merlyn, *The Execution (Death of Mussolini)*, 1945, Oil, $32\frac{1}{4} \times 46\frac{1}{2}$ ins

symbolic and macabre billet for licentious soldiery in general. *Soldiers at Rye* is a powerful and imaginative painting of a kind far removed from the on-the-spot reportage that was within the range of most war artists. Burra was only 37 when he painted this picture but his health, after a childhood attack of rheumatic fever, was never such as to have made any active part in the war possible.

Charles Ginner, a painter of an earlier generation to Burra's, and who only just survived the war, produced one exceptionally fine oil, *Building a Battleship*. In such pictures as Burra's and Ginner's the essential characteristics of painters with achieved styles take on fresh contexts.

# Sources and Select Bibliography

All quotations, where not acknowledged in the text, come from either letters from the artists concerned to the Secretary of the War Artists' Advisory Committee, held in the archives of the Imperial War Museum, or from recorded interviews, *Artists in an Age of Conflict*, made by the Imperial War Museum, Department of Sound Records. There are no books to my knowledge dealing comprehensively with the art of the Second World War, but the following contain references to the war paintings of individual artists.

Betjeman, John, *John Piper*, Penguin, 1946

Blake, John, (Introduction by), *The Aviation Art of Frank Wootton*, Peacock Press, 1976

Bowness, Alan, *William Scott*, Lund Humphries, 1964

Carline, Richard, and Causey, Andrew, *Stanley Spencer*, Royal Academy Catalogue, Weidenfeld and Nicolson, 1980

Causey, Andrew, *Paul Nash*, Tate Gallery, 1975

Cooper, Douglas, *Sutherland*, Lund Humphries, 1961

Cork, Richard, *Vorticism*, Gordon Fraser, 1976

*Richard Eurich*, Imperial War Museum Catalogue

Freer, Allen, *The Rose of Death: Albert Richards*, Arts Council–Imperial War Museum, 1978

Gowing, Lawrence, *William Coldstream* (Catalogue), Arts Council, 1962

*Anthony Gross: India in Action*, National Gallery Catalogue

Hall, Donald, *Henry Moore*, Gollancz, 1966

Harrison, Charles, *English Art and Modernism 1900–39*, Allen Lane, 1981

Hedgecoe, John, *Henry Moore*, Nelson, 1968

*Thomas Hennell: Watercolours 1941–45*, Imperial War Museum Catalogue

Lipke, William, *David Bomberg*, Evelyn, Adams and Mackay, 1967

Michel, Walter, *Wyndham Lewis*, Thames and Hudson, 1971

*Eric Ravilious: Watercolours 1940–42*, Imperial War Museum Catalogue

Richards, J.M., *Edward Bawden*, Penguin, 1946

Rothenstein, John, *Modern English Painters*, rev. ed., 3 vols, Macdonald and Jane's, 1976

Tassi, Roberto, *Sutherland: the wartime drawings*, Sotheby/Parke Bernet, 1980

West, Anthony, *John Piper*, Secker and Warburg, 1979

White, Gabriel, *Edward Ardizzone*, Bodley Head, 1979

# Acknowledgments

For permission to reproduce copyright material in the book the author and publishers are grateful to the following: George Allen & Unwin Ltd, for extracts on pp. 36, 120 and 153 from *Raider's Dawn* (1942) and *Ha! Ha! Among the Trumpets* (1944) by Alun Lewis; Anvil Press Poetry Ltd/Menard Press, for passages on pp. 22 and 53 from F.T. Prince's *Collected Poems* (1978); the estate of the late Jocelyn Brooke, for the lines on p. 158 from 'Landscape near Tobruk' which appeared in *December Spring* published by Bodley Head (1946); Jonathan Cape Ltd, for the extracts on pp. 11 and 125 from Henry Reed's *A Map of Verona* (1946); Chatto & Windus Ltd (on behalf of the Author's Literary Estate), for the lines on pp. 50 and 133 from *Collected Poems* by Norman Cameron (1942), and for the extract on p. 63 from *Collected Poems* by Richard Eberhart (1960); Andre Deutsch Ltd, for extracts on pp. 66, 95 and 145 from *Collected Poems* by Roy Fuller (1962); Faber and Faber Ltd and Farrar, Straus & Giroux Inc., for extracts on pp. 72 ('The Death of the Ball-Turret Gunner') and 167 (excerpt from 'The Dead Wingman') taken from *Randall Jarrell: The Complete Poems* (Copyright © 1945, 1969 by Mrs Randall Jarrell; copyright renewed © 1972 by Mrs Randall Jarrell); also Faber and Faber Ltd and Harcourt Brace Jovanovich Inc., for lines on p. 57 from *Poems 1943–56* by Richard Wilbur (1957); Professor Norman Hampson, for lines on p. 86 from his poem 'Assault Convoy'; Hutchinson Publishing Group Ltd, for the poem on p. 178 from *Collected Poems* by Gavin Ewart (1980); London Magazine Editions, for extracts on pp. 42, 113 and 149 taken from *Old Damson Face* by Bernard Gutteridge (1975); Lund Humphries Publishers, London, for material on pp. 36 and 48 reproduced from *Sutherland* by Douglas Cooper (1961); Macmillan Publishers Ltd, for the extracts on pp. 86 and 162 taken from *Collected Poems* by Charles Causley (1953); Oxford University Press, for lines on pp. 8, 101, 139 and 173 from *The Complete Poems of Keith Douglas*, edited by Desmond Graham (1978); Routledge & Kegan Paul Ltd, for lines reproduced on pp. 129 and 184 from *Indian Landscape* by R.N. Curry (1947).

For permission to reproduce colour plates the author and publishers are grateful to: the Royal Air Force Museum, Hendon, section centrefold between pp. 132 and 133, below left; the Tate Gallery, London, section centrefold between pp. 60 and 61, below. The remaining colour plates are reproduced by courtesy of the Imperial War Museum, London.

Black and white illustrations appear by kind permission of the following: Astley Hall, Chorley, p. 74; Bendigo Art Gallery, Victoria, Australia, p. 85; Bradford Art Gallery and Museums, p. 119; the City of Bristol Museum and Art Gallery, pp. 49, 51, 127; the British Council, p. 152; Castlemaine Art Gallery, Victoria, Australia, p. 142; Glasgow Art Gallery and Museum, pp. 40, 41; Government Art Collection, p. 122; Harris Museum and Art Gallery, Preston, p. 16; Launceston Gallery, Tasmania, p. 65 below; Leeds City Art Galleries, pp. 31, 75; City of Manchester Art Gallery, pp. 77, 175; Manchester Education Committee, p. 128; Henry Moore Foundation, p. 40; Rodrigo Moynihan, p. 131; National Gallery of Canada, Ottawa, pp. 23, 65 above, 93, 180 above; National Maritime Museum, London, pp. 114, 163, 171 below, 176, 185; Private Collection, p. 126; the Royal Pavilion, Art Gallery and Museums, Brighton, pp. 92, 150; Russell-Cotes Art Gallery and Museum, Bournemouth, p. 109; Salford Art Gallery and Museum, pp. 68, 70; William Scott, p. 125; South African National Gallery, pp. 71 above, 140; Southampton Art Gallery and Museums, p. 117; the Tate Gallery, London, pp. 38, 43, 58, 79, 87, 96, 131, 161, 186; Wakefield Art Gallery and Museums, p.45; Walker Art Gallery, Liverpool, p. 108. The remaining pictures belong to the collection at the Imperial War Museum, to which we make due acknowledgment. The pictures on pp. 33, 67, 88, 90 and 172 were destroyed by enemy action.

# Index

Note: Page numbers in bold refer to b/w illustrations, those in italics refer to colour plates